BELIEVE
In What You
SEE

KNOWING GOD PERSONALLY BY
SEEING HIS PRESENCE IN NATURE

DEBBIE FEYH

CITI OF
BOOKS

CITIOFBOOKS, INC.
3736 Eubank NE Suite A1
Albuquerque, NM 87111-3579
www.citiofbooks.com
Hotline: 1 (877) 389-2759
Fax: 1 (505) 930-7244

Ordering Information:
Quantity sales. Special discounts are available on quantity purchases by corporations, associations, and others. For details, contact the publisher at the address above.

Printed in the United States of America.
ISBN-13:   Paperback   979-8-90124-223-0
                    eBook   979-8-90124-225-4
                    Hardback   979-8-90124-224-7

Discover the Benefits Waiting for You.

www.GoExperienceNature.com

To the reader,

I pray that you feel the heart and soul of your Almighty Creator on every page of this book as you learn to recognize and experience His glorious presence in nature, forever beside and all around you, 24-7.

The heavens declare the glory of God, and the skies announce what his hands have made. Day after day they tell the story; night after night they tell it again. They have no speech or words; they have no voice to be heard. But their message goes out through all the world; their words go everywhere on earth. The sky is like a home for the sun.

—Psalm 19:1–4

CONTENTS

INTRODUCTION

The Answer to Your Worries Might Surprise You

Do you desperately want to see God? The answer to your desperation might surprise you.

Nature glorifies God's presence so you can see and hear Him anytime, any day, anywhere in the world.

"The heavens declare the glory of God, and the skies announce what His hands have made" (Psalm 19:1).

You and every living thing want to be known and loved. The sun, trees, zebras, stars, and tulips all trust God, the maker of the waves, to provide for their needs.

God continually sees and cares for you and them, showing His incredible heart of love for you daily throughout creation. God's presence is glorified at all times in His plan for nature.

When I was ten years old, my uncle was killed in a farming accident, and it changed everything for our family. I learned at a young age that your life can be turned upside down in a moment.

When you experience loss, you feel so overwhelmed and wonder if God sees you, is near, or even cares. Processing the fear of reality or the unknown can make you doubt who God really is. Fear can make you question your beliefs, purpose, and the plan for you on this earth.

Where is God when you need Him, and why can't you see Him? What problems do you need God to solve for you?

Every person who lives on earth experiences heartache and

sadness. After the accident, I was mad at God. I folded Him neatly into a box and determined who I thought He was. Can you relate? Have you ever put God in a box?

The Bible talks about a man named Job who simultaneously lost his family, livestock, and everything he owned. Job never gave up on God. Throughout the chapters of this book, you will learn many lessons from Job regarding coping with the sadness you might feel when life just isn't going how you want it to go.

Some days, living life might make you feel as fabulous and colorful as the sunrise it began with. Other days may be complicated and leave you feeling as dark as the night that follows the day. God allows you to experience hard times so you will learn to look for His presence and lean on Him to find purpose.

God named and designed nature to supply everything you need to rock this one precious life you are gifted with. Nature is God's life-processing form of CPR.

God's plan for creation is a **P**rocess that **C**onnects God's assigned **P**urpose of **R**epeating His love and presence over and over for you to see. Your heavenly Father formed you with a purpose and has assigned you and me as caretakers of the earth. Is your purpose something you ponder?

Nature teaches that the purpose of life is a life of purpose.

Several years after the dreadful accident that took my uncle's life, Grandma asked me a question while we were feeding cows in the pasture. Her question stirred my heart while changing my disbelieving perspective.

Now, I view nature's purpose, process, and connection as traits of God's character. Changing my perspective changed my heart to believe in what I see, and I want to share this outlook with you.

Nature is God's life-processing form of CPR. Through PCPR, you will see the presence of God for yourself in creation, viewing the possibilities of a world you have lived in but may have never considered.

What fears can you let lose when witnessing God's presence in creation? How will your faith and trust grow? Discovering God's presence in nature can equip you to let go of your worries and fears, unearthing your unique purpose.

You don't get to decide what thunderstorms life will blow your way, but you can determine how you take cover and deal with them (Psalm 91:4). What is in your heart? Will you use heartache as an excuse or a hopeful motivation?

This book will make you think. It will show you ways to see God's creative presence in nature near you right now, anywhere outside your front door or under God's beautiful blue sky.

Your perspective of God and the earth you live on will change, making you think about God as if there are no boxes.

The more you look for God and focus on His plan, the easier He is to see. This will encourage you to realize that creation is so impressive it could only be from God. You can trust and believe in God's plan.

Seeing isn't always believing, but believing is how you will see.

CHAPTER 1

WHERE IS GOD?

hat do you think is God's favorite color? My grandma asked me this question one day when I was about fifteen years old, and it absolutely changed my life.

At that point, my picture of God was of a little old man with white hair and a long beard. He was crotchety and sat on a rock in the clouds, making up rules for me to follow. I felt like He wanted to control people's lives, and I didn't appreciate it.

I saw God as someone who hurt people because I'd witnessed and lived through it.

Today, I know that God wasn't out to get me. He doesn't actually keep score, but at one point, I believed that.

So how about you? Have you ever felt like asking God, "What is this? Why are You allowing this? What are You doing?"

Maybe it's because you had a falling out with a friend group, or you lost that dream job or a relationship with someone you loved. Or you have a story like mine.

I was raised on a farm. When I was in the fourth grade, my uncle, who was loved dearly by our family, by his community, and by his church, was killed on the farm during harvest.

When you grow up on a farm, death is a part of your

everyday life. Animals are born, and animals die. But I quickly realized that when people die, it's way different.

My uncle was only thirty-two years old and had a young family. He loved the Lord and faithfully served at our church. He encouraged kids in children's church to memorize Bible verses, and when we did, he took us out for ice cream.

My dad, grandpa, and uncle each owned separate farms and livestock, but they farmed together and helped one another out. My uncle's death changed everything for our family.

I learned life is imperfect, even when you share it with Jesus. You see, about three months before the accident, I had made my way to the altar in children's church and given Jesus my heart.

I assumed the grief I was dealing with was handed to me by God. I blamed God. I asked God why He let this awful situation occur and why it had happened to my family and me. I felt like God was ignoring me when I didn't get any answers.

I believed I couldn't and shouldn't trust God. I mean, He let my family down in a big way. He let Uncle Roger die while working hard on his farm, even though he served God faithfully. Where was God when my uncle needed him? Why would He allow this to happen?

I didn't understand God and decided that I didn't want anything to do with Him. If that was the kind of God He was, I was out. I gave up on God. I walked away from God because I didn't trust His plan; I would make my own and didn't need Him.

Have you been there? Have you ever felt ignored by God? Sometimes, life can be tricky. Sadness and grief can be overwhelming.

On a typical day, you mainly deal with small amounts of emotion at a time. But when discouragement and grief occur, there are so many more emotions for you to deal with, an overload all at once.

Your head and heart may feel saturated with sadness. Losing something or someone dear to your heart can cause fear, anger, and disappointment to overcome your thoughts, making the mind overwhelmed and confused.

When feeling scared, you seek relief from your emotions. The weight of dealing with difficult times and painful situations can knock you off your feet, causing you to crumble to your knees. Sometimes, you might cry out for help into what can seem like endless darkness. At that moment, God can seem unreachable.

Have you been there? Have you ever felt ignored by God or questioned where He is?

You and I talk to ourselves more than anyone else. Instead of using facts, our minds will concoct stories that are not true. We can get lost in a hopeless struggle when we focus on ourselves and forget to connect with God's presence in our surroundings.

Emotions take over our thoughts, only increasing the stress in our minds, situations, and relationships.

The book of Job describes a prosperous man of God who lost his possessions, children, and health. An influential man, Job possessed admirable character and loved God. Job longed to understand why he was suffering, and he argued his case. "Everything I feared and dreaded has happened to me. I have no peace or quietness. I have no rest, only trouble" (Job 3:25–26). Job struggled to understand why these circumstances were happening to him.

Why is it that when things are going well, we pat ourselves on the back for doing such a good job, but when situations in life head south and go badly, we blame God for being in complete control?

When our lives fall apart, we automatically transfer the responsibility of life back to God, accusing the Creator of causing the problem. We attribute our troubles to God, letting fear grip our minds as it manipulates all the possible outcomes spinning around in our grief-stricken brains.

I blamed God. I was scared and assumed the grief I was dealing with was handed to me by God. I felt invisible.

When our minds get the best of us, entangled thoughts cause us to completely forget that God is right there, waiting with a plan to guide, direct, and help. "For I am the Lord, your God, who takes hold of your right hand and says to you, do not fear; I will help you" (Isaiah 41:13). God is our only hope.

You can count on God because He is alive and well. He understands your every word, experiences your every emotion, and hears your desperate prayers. God will help you release your fear as He holds your hand. Reread Isaiah 41:13 and let it soak in.

After my uncle's heart-wrenching accident, we hung out at Grandpa and Grandma's house for several days. Friends, family, and neighbors visited and brought loads of food. On Sunday, we went to church.

I really didn't want to go and had many thoughts running in my head. Why would God let Uncle Roger die? What kind of a person was God? Did He not understand the pain I was feeling?

Our church family connected with us and helped to carry the burden of our feelings through their tears. The people of the church joined us in the grieving process. The pastor prayed and wept. The congregation prayed, hugged, and loved us.

Even at the young age of ten, I could feel the genuine compassion the church poured into our family. I was trying to deal with my emotions of grief, anger, and disappointment. I had so many feelings that I just didn't know what to do with them. So, as many of us do, I pushed them down deep, hoping they would go away.

I was a child at that point, so I thought like a child. Today, as a grown woman, many years after the accident, I still don't understand that part of God's plan, and I still don't like it.

But I do know that God is not a vengeful God. He doesn't intentionally harm people or take loved ones away out of spite. He loves you, sees you, and has a plan for you.

How you learn to process the purpose of hurt and pain as a child can determine how you process issues and emotions over time as an adult.

Trying to push away your feelings is a terrible plan. Feeling your feelings is important because it allows you to process and understand them so that they don't turn into a bigger problem.

Events that happen during childhood can shape you into who you are as an adult. Childhood memories become an integral part of your story, a process that connects you to the very fiber of your being.

Living life seems to follow the same plan as nature. Everything is a process. Nothing is instantaneous.

There are hardly words to describe the pain when your best friend commits suicide hours after you leave his house or the father and young son of the family you nanny for are killed in a car wreck. As a child or an adult, it can be difficult to express how you feel in times of heartache. Time does not stop, waiting for you to heal. You must continue life, existing hour by hour, day by day.

Sometimes, your own friends and family can unknowingly make the situation harder for you. Others probably won't understand what you are feeling and thinking. But God does, and His presence in creation will always encompass you.

You can feel God's love in the warm sunshine on your skin

and see Him in the beauty of a butterfly as it travels from plant to plant. Only God knows what is in your mind and heart as He holds your hand, reminding you not to be afraid.

Do you ever ask others to pray for you, thinking they might do a better job? God just wants you to talk with Him. You don't need to pray a big, fancy prayer. Simply speak to God from your heart, and He will listen.

My grandma was a beautifully strong Christian woman with a bit of mischief in her soul. She read her Bible often and seemed to have a direct line to God. When she prayed, it was as if God came down and filled the room with His presence.

Knowing Grandma's gift, I felt I didn't need to pray for anything. When I had prayer requests regarding essential things in my life, I would tell Grandma and ask her to pray.

After my uncle's accident, I had so many feelings to deal with and didn't know what to do with them. I didn't know how to talk with God, and I didn't tell anyone else because I knew my family was dealing with their own hurts. All those feelings I had stuffed down deep didn't go away.

So when Grandma asked me, "Deb, what do you think is God's favorite color?" I couldn't even answer her because I had never thought about God like that. I had always kept God in a box with a tight lid on it. I wanted to determine who He was. I had my own plan and didn't want to follow His.

If your heart is full of anger, disappointment, and trouble, those bad things will block your eyes from focusing on the connection of good things in nature. You won't be able to witness the purpose and process of what God has in store for you, the many blessings waiting for you in the great outdoors (1 Peter 5:7). The feelings and emotions held captive in your heart will determine how you see God's presence near you.

Take time to find someone safe you can talk with to process and discuss your feelings. God will help you through the process, but you must be willing to deal with the issue. Feel the feelings.

Connect with God to let go of your hurt and pain so you won't be continually carrying it around. Many counselors and resources are available to help guide you through the process. Healing the heart takes time and effort. It's not an overnight fix.

You don't get to choose what tornadoes of life hurl your way, but you can decide how you view the colors of the sunset. You might not be able to control what is happening, but you can choose how the hardships of life will affect you.

Bad things can determine how you live the process of life, but only if you let them. Life can be hard and cause fear, but there is always hope when you continually see God's presence beside you in nature (Joshua 1:7–9).

God's overwhelming presence occurs and exists on earth 24-7. He is always present to comfort you. Even though you cannot physically see Him with your eyes, you can continually feel the safety of His presence. The Almighty Creator is always beside, around, and among us.

What is beautiful to you? What gives you hope?

Sometimes, it's the little things in life that make them so special. Like watching a bee collect nectar while moving from flower to flower, hearing the leaves on a tree overhead rustle in the wind, or naming the shapes of the white, puffy clouds in the beautiful blue sky. Savor that quality time with God.

God's existence is visible throughout the world, especially in the beautiful things of nature. Cherish the moments when you know you are seeing God.

Looking for God in creation daily will remind you that He is always nearby (Lamentations 3:22–23). You can lean on God's tangible existence to live life and rest in His love.

God didn't put you on earth to deal with life alone. You can read the Bible for ways to see the glory of God's presence. "All scripture is breathed out by God" (2 Timothy 3:16).

God breathed His breath into Adam, which means that those who penned the Bible were not only created by God, but God also inspired the scriptures.

By the end of this book, you will learn how to connect creation to your way of life and recognize the blue and green of God's plan. Expect God, and He will meet you. He is always with you if you look. He is a constant friend with whom you can share and talk.

God is active and will be wherever you allow him to be (Deuteronomy 31:6). God's plan revolves around His people getting to know Him.

Points to Ponder

Who is God to you? Do you see and feel His presence?

CHAPTER 2

DOES GOD HAVE A FAVORITE COLOR?

*S*ometimes, you don't know what you don't know until someone teaches or mentors you, showing you how to think differently. My grandma helped me see God differently in the middle of a pasture.

For more than sixty years, Grandpa and Grandma owned a dairy. An average of one hundred dairy cows would walk through the concrete barn daily, beginning at 3:00 a.m. and 3:00 p.m. I started helping with the evening milking when I was going into the seventh grade.

Around 2:00 p.m. each day, Grandpa or I would ride the four-wheeler into the pasture to bring in the cows. We would herd the big black-and-white Holstein cows into a secure holding pen behind the milk barn.

Then Grandpa would fire up the hay monster (the coolest hay mover ever) and drive us out to the pasture. Grandma and I would sit toward the back, daydreaming, chitchatting, and sharing our thoughts during the ride.

On this particular day, I was strategically perched on a stack of small, green, square alfalfa hay bales beside Grandma. We bounced along, riding on the back of the hay monster on our way to feed the cows. Above us, an eminent sky presented a magnificent shade of ocean blue.

It was the perfect setting for a life lesson to jump into my day unexpectedly. Have you been there? You know, the kind of inspiration that hits you upside your head before you even realize what just happened.

The hot afternoon wind felt like someone had opened a mammoth clothes dryer's door. The tortoise-speed ride was bumpy as we bounced over mounds of dirt created by prairie dogs. The wind carried the sweet aroma of freshly cut alfalfa, which smelled strong and pungent.

The vast sea of unending open sky was a gorgeous shade of bright blue. There was not a white, puffy cloud to be seen. The tall forest-green cottonwood trees stood strong along the edge of the pasture, perfectly framing the bottom outline of a picturesque endless pool of blue sky. An infinite sea of life-giving emerald grass filled the pasture, making the picture complete.

While contently daydreaming in my own little world, Grandma tenderly laid her hand on my arm to draw my attention. As our eyes met, her gaze was intense. Looking deep into my eyes, Grandma searched my soul for answers. Then she asked a question that would eventually change my life.

Drawing me into her thoughts, Grandma asked, "Deb, what do you think is God's favorite color?" I turned to face her as my blue eyes met Grandma's green.

I'll be honest. My first thought was, *What? I'm over here thinking about important things, and that's all you got?*

But her gaze seemed to search deep into my young soul. Grandma had a gift. She could look into my eyes and read my thoughts like a book. She knew my mind was churning, and I had no words. With a sly little grin, she whispered, "It must be blue and green."

She pointed at the beautiful blue sky and exclaimed, "Deb, it couldn't get much bluer than this." She described how everything was green as far as the eye could see—waving her arm out in front of her like a magic wand. My eyes scanned the broad path that her arm had traveled, soaking in the colors before me.

Now, I am a logical person. I like to think things through. I want to see facts that practice common sense, and Grandma wasn't wrong. Everything around me, from ground to sky, was a magnificent shade of blue or green.

Have you ever asked yourself if the Almighty Creator has favorite colors? When you go outside, what colors do you see the most of?

After Grandma asked me about God's favorite color, my mind raced wildly, thinking, *Is God actually someone who would have a favorite color? Does the little old grouchy dude even care about colors?*

At this point, my mind screeched. *Wait, what?* When I looked out across the pasture, blue and green were all I could see. Grandma's question was such a profound thought, like God was essentially a person with a personality. I had never considered God like that.

I saw acres and acres of green grass with wildflowers dancing in the breeze. There were large groves of big, giant cottonwood trees with their leaves blowing and clapping in the wind. Above us was an endless ocean of beautiful blue. Everything I could see was bathed in gorgeous shades of blue and green.

My mind could hardly wrap itself around the fact that I had sat in this same spot and traveled this same exact path to feed cows in the pasture so many times. Yet I had never seen or experienced what I was seeing right now.

When I focused on the nature around me and looked for God's favorite colors, blue and green were everywhere. Wow! I was simply amazed. It was like the earth had actually been decorated with a color scheme.

I was dumbfounded. I looked back over Grandma and didn't say a thing because I couldn't. It was like my mind was in overdrive. I was in awe of what she had just pointed out to me.

I knew God created everything. I mean, ever since I was born, I had heard that. But that thought to me had always been like a head thing, a fact. I wasn't walking with God at this point and never thought about Him.

As my eyes focused on the vast ocean of blue sky above and the endless span of green pasture grasses waving in the wind before me, Grandma spoke again. With a twinkle in her eye, she pounded the nail in on her thoughts, adding the fact that water and oceans are blue as well.

Grandma tenderly placed her hand on my arm. Leaning close to my face, she whispered slowly and intently, "Deb, God created all of this, and He loves you. Believe in what you see."

Have you ever been speechless? Have you ever realized the beauty of God's presence in nature and your mind could not wrap itself around the situation enough to even respond? That is the awe of God.

Grandma's words instantly seeped deep into my soul, raising the hair on the back of my neck. Even though I was sitting in the hot sun, every bone in my body quivered, knowing she spoke the truth. I felt as if the stars seemed to align.

All the scripture readings, Sunday school teachings, and sermons I had heard at church over the years all seemed to stream together in my mind all at once. A tremendous, overwhelming feeling I had never encountered before bathed every inch of my body. I felt as if I had just gulped down a large bottle of cold water, and it plunged into my every limb. The lightning-fast feeling scared me!

Grandma's uncanny awareness of our colorful surroundings was spot-on. Dumbfounded and stumbling to find words, I nodded my head while mumbling some form of agreement.

Thankfully, the hay monster had stopped, and it was time to break the bales. I jumped to my feet and went to work quickly. My overwhelmed mind welcomed the physical work.

Silver pliers breaking the metal wires on the bales created a sharp clicking sound, followed by a whoosh sound as bright green flakes of hay tumbled into the bottoms of large iron cattle feeders. Over and over again, the rhythm of pliers breaking wire and the broken bales tumbling could be heard. The sweet smell of fresh alfalfa for one hundred cows drifted through the air. Finally, the hay monster was empty of its bales.

Standing on the deck of the hay monster beside the full feeders, I paused for a moment, taking in my surroundings. Sucking in a deep breath of pasture, fresh oxygen, laced with sweet alfalfa. I could feel the beauty of nature surrounding me, soaking into every cell of my body.

While standing on the hay monster looking out across the pasture, deep down in my soul, I knew I had been judging God unfairly. I needed to adjust my view of Him and try looking from a different angle.

I needed to stop continually looking up at Him through my pain, which only clouded my vision. I needed to look toward God through the beauty of nature and His creation.

If God designed and created all this beauty, His heart must also be in nature, right? I love the colors, smells, sounds, and feelings I experience outdoors. My favorite place to be is outside in nature. So I started thinking, *Maybe He's not so different from me after all. Perhaps I should give Him a second chance and look more at His plan instead of mine.*

Grandma's question caused me to think about where God is and who He is differently, completely blowing the lid off the box that I had folded God up in.

Have you ever felt your perspective change as you looked over a situation? As your mind begins to comprehend what your eyes are telling you? It can be amazing and overwhelming all at once.

As Grandpa drove us back to the barn, I spotted three does startled by the commotion in their territory bounding across the seemingly infinite green pasture. With their white tails bouncing, the deer gracefully cleared the five-strand barbed-wire fence without effort.

Plump wild turkeys were feasting in the field beside us. Hesitating for a moment, the turkeys observed the deer activity. Seemingly unthreatened by the commotion, the tom turkey continued strutting his stuff. He was showing off his plumage and colors, trying to impress his lady friends with his handsome tail feathers fanned.

As I watched the process of the wildlife display unfold before my eyes, it occurred to me that God created all of this on purpose with a purpose. The amazing beauty in nature we witness daily is repetitively fashioned and connected for a reason.

I began to see God with a new viewpoint framed with a much kinder picture. All I could think of was, *Why had I never connected God and nature before now?*

Why had I never given God credit for the amazing colors of a peacock's feathers or the smell of a sweet red rose? Why had I never linked the glorious beauty of a horse as it glides across the pasture, galloping with its main and tail blowing in the wind, back to God and His plan?

Then it hit me. I was angry with God. I was the one holding out. I couldn't see because of me. God wasn't hiding from me. His nearness was waiting to be seen by me.

How are you feeling? Does the idea of God ever feel overwhelming to you? Sometimes, does He seem like just too much? Do you have God in a box?

I had been carrying this grudge against God for years and totally missed seeing His glory in nature. Honestly, I had never even realized that I felt this way. Observing the fantastic beauty before me, I knew there was much more to God's presence here than meets the eye. I needed to look harder.

Have you ever been mad or upset with God? Are you willing to admit it? Do you recognize your thoughts and feelings toward Him? How do you mentally fold God up?

The Bible describes Job as a wealthy farmer living in the land of Uz (Job 1:1). His occupation was growing food for his family and workers, and his everyday life revolved around the weather and God's timing.

Imagine Job peacefully resting in his favorite chair at home when several messengers came running in (Job 1:14–18). They were beside themselves, waving their hands while anxiously trying to explain the catastrophic events they had witnessed. The attacks from the Sabeans were like seeing lightning falling from the sky.

After all the stories were told, Job had lost everything. Job got up, tore his robe, shaved his head, and bowed down to the ground to worship God.

Even after everything in his life had fallen apart, Job never gave up on God. Job trusted God wholeheartedly and focused on God instead of his distress and troubles.

Job said, "I was naked when I was born, and I will be naked when I die. The Lord gave these things to me, and he has taken them away. Praise the name of the Lord. In all this, Job did not sin or blame God" (Job 1:21–22).

Loving and following God does not provide you protection from difficulties. Disappointment, loss of loved ones, and troubled relationships still happen.

Understanding why you must experience troubles is hard, but the experience can lead you to a much stronger and closer trusting relationship with your heavenly Father. Focusing on God during heartache will grow your faith by teaching you to lean into Him and learn more about Him. Don't give up on God's plan.

Things don't seem real until they get personal, right? Situations affect how you live when they intermingle with your feelings and emotions. Your perspective may change or adjust to the challenge. God can help you shift your perspective and move forward gracefully.

How about you? What are you doing with all those feelings you have stuffed down deep, trying to hide? God loves you. He sees you. Trust God and give Him all those yucky feelings in your heart so He can help you to get rid of them.

God is always bigger than the box we fold him up into. Think about God like there is no box.

Your perspective regarding the God of creation will change your faith and how you live. Do you recognize or admit God's presence is always near you in nature? Do you trust God to do what is best for you?

Perspective can be like a pair of glasses, a view designed uniquely for our eyes based on many life experiences. If you and I swapped glasses, my eyes would not see what you see, and you would not see what I see.

Not only do our eyes see differently, but our minds and hearts experience situations differently as well, causing you and me to have unique and different perspectives based on our life events.

When I stood on the hay monster looking out over the pasture, I felt as if I were looking through a new pair of God's glasses that showed how He sees creation. Looking down from God's viewpoint on the beauty surrounding me was all new. The disappointment I had been carrying around in my heart for years was overshadowed and covered by all the brilliant aspects and colors of nature before me.

My eyes were opened to the purpose of God's beauty. I felt true joy, like a toddler experiencing something new for the first time. This magnificent realization changed my perspective of who God is forever. Since that day, I have never looked at the purpose and process of God or nature the same way again (Lamentations 3:24).

Why did Grandma's simple question cause such perplexing thoughts in my mind? It was the first time in my life that I was struck with awe at the picturesque beauty surrounding me. My heart and soul genuinely began to believe God is real, and I live in His story. Feeling God's love changed me.

From that day on, Grandma mentored me daily. She taught me to take the time to recognize God's presence in creation and ponder God's remarkable miracles that constantly surround me in nature. I learned to notice the beautiful sunlight streaming through the trees, recognize unique patterns and colors wildflowers wear, and love the smell of rain.

Grandma always asked me, "Did you see that?" when I arrived at work to milk. "Did you catch God's sunset last night? Did you notice the colorful leaves on the trees on the way over? Did you see God's beautiful wildflowers blooming in the field in front of the house when you drove in?" She kept me on my toes.

God designed nature to show you His presence while

growing your faith and trust in Him. Twenty-four seven, God reveals himself to you. The process of nature is one of God's most beautiful creations, teaching us to believe in what we see. A glorious gift deliberately connected and planned for you to benefit mentally and physically, and learn to trust Him on a personal level.

Once you see God's incredible presence in the beauty of the great outdoors, you almost can't unsee it. Shifting your focus will awaken a new awareness of nature around you.

Do you ever really think about that? I didn't.

Realizing that God is right here with you in your everyday life might be a new concept to grasp. Emanuel means God is with us (Matthew 1:23). The beauty in your surroundings is a constant reminder that God is near no matter what county, city, state, country, or continent you are standing in.

Grandma told me, "Deb, no matter where you go, there you are, and God is always with you." Honestly, it took me years to understand that. But it means God's presence is always with you in the beauty of nature wherever you go, no matter where you are on this earth. Trust in His plan.

"Seek beauty everywhere" (Doris Day).

Once you recognize God's glorious, intrinsic beauty, you can't unsee it, nor do you want to. What blue is to the sky is God's intrinsic glory. What wet is to water is God's intrinsic glory.

Do you connect God as being the total creative source of everything? God created nature to show His presence as part of the rhythm of your daily life.

My farming family has planted fields of seeds my entire life. I watched the seeds mature into adult plants. Then we harvest the crops, providing food and seeds for the following year, a process that outlines God's life-giving purpose of taking care of His people from nature generation after generation.

Have you witnessed the miraculous process and excitement of new life born as live baby animals are born on the farm? Or maybe the birth of your children? Let your mind connect God to the purpose of nature.

Every unique detail in the process of creation proclaims God's heart. He will fill your heart as you slow down to smell and discover the incredible beauty of His creation. God never leaves you.

Do you look for Him? God is everywhere. Everything you see in nature is His design. Sunflowers, cedar trees, black-and-white cows, and the blue sky announce God's glory. Open your eyes, mind, and heart to see His presence. Looking for God every day will affect your head and your heart.

Let me say that again: seeing God every day and looking for Him beyond yourself will affect how you feel about God in your head and your heart.

Nature is like God hollering, "Here I am!" making God seem almost tangible, like holding a leaf from a tree is like touching God's hand. The leaf isn't God, but it shows His undeniable presence. God's fingerprint is on the beauty of all creation (Psalm 8:3).

One of the most reliable ways to see God's existence is to see His presence in the beauty of nature, displaying His power, creativity, and wisdom. God's ingenious work of creation is an ongoing, never-ending process.

Creation promises hope while guiding you toward experiencing true trust and finding your unique purpose (Psalm 119:90).

Where have you experienced God's incomprehensible presence in your life? Try keeping a God's Presence Diary. Jot down the experience so that you won't forget it.

Record where you see the Almighty Hand of God's presence working. On days you question where God is, read what God has done for you in the past.

Alter how you look at life by looking for God's incredible artistic creations in nature.

Gain a new perspective, bringing your relationship with God closer than ever. Study your surroundings and realize that each day with God's presence is extraordinary.

Points to Ponder

What are your biggest fears?

CHAPTER 3

WHAT YOU LISTEN FOR IS WHAT YOU HEAR

*G*od places other people in your life at just the right time to help you adjust your perspective.

Growing up, the church was comfortable, and I was there often. Participating in the youth group was a blast. I felt loved by my family, friends, and church people. However, a close relationship with God was unknown to me.

Something about Him just seemed so distant, far away, and overwhelming. Can you relate? Have you ever felt that way?

I didn't communicate with God much and never read my Bible. I respected Him. I believed He was the Creator and real. I never doubted that. I tried to follow His rules, but we didn't have a relationship. I attended church faithfully and sang the songs, but I didn't know God.

A new pastor moved into the church parsonage. Two of Pastor Crosley's kids were in high school, and their ages were close to mine. We became instant friends.

Randy was three years older than me. He began working

with my brother and cousins on our summer hay crew. Reverend Crosley, who grew up on a farm, was overly excited to visit Randy at work.

The preacher possessed a smile that could light up a room. Not knowing a stranger, he could talk with anyone and was friends with everyone. When speaking, he looked directly into your eyes. He was totally present, all there. You could feel him listening to what you were saying. He was so laid back and different from the other pastors I had known.

One afternoon, the new pastor showed up at Grandpa and Grandma's farm while we were doing chores. He was sporting khaki pants covered with paint stains and plenty of holes. The pants were paired with a white T-shirt chockfull of holes as well. A floppy tan hat that had seen better days accentuated his outfit. He looked like a mess but wore a smile that portrayed genuine joy and excitement. Returning to his childhood days on the farm, he was thrilled to be outside in the sunshine.

I was shocked. This was the first pastor who had ever come out to visit. It was hard to believe this bum-looking guy was the same guy who stood behind the pulpit on Sundays wearing a suit and tie.

I lived a sheltered small-town farm life. Reverend Crosley was the closest person to a celebrity I had ever known. On Sunday mornings, this man preached from the pulpit to more than three hundred people.

Can you relate? We didn't go to concerts or even surf the internet. Hanging with family was our entertainment.

Reverend Crosley asked Grandpa if he could come out another day to help milk cows. I sensed this was only the beginning of the new pastor's visits.

So, on a beautiful afternoon in July, Pastor Crosley showed up to help milk cows. Seated on a wooden stool in the pit of the milking parlor, he wore a huge smile that beamed across his face, indicating he was thrilled to be a part of the action.

The milk barn is a quiet and somber place. Cows need to be very calm and tranquil to let their milk down. The only constant noise heard is the humming of the milk machines and an old radio station playing classic Johnny Cash, Conway Twitty, and George Jones.

I might be a bit partial, but I have to say the ladies had good taste. They loved classic country.

The preacher looked so content sitting on the barstool— no worries, like he had all the time in the world. The cows didn't recognize the pastor's voice, so he whispered most of his comments, trying to be as quiet as possible.

Using my own version of sign language, I offered to teach the preacher how to milk a cow. Declining the offer, he was content to sit on the stool and watch.

A new cow entered the barn to be milked, and Grandma promptly introduced her to the pastor. She was Grandma's favorite cow. The sweet cow was named Barbara in honor of his wife, Mrs. Crosley. The pastor was beyond thrilled.

From then on, when a cow entered the barn, he would ask the cow's name. Grandma would introduce him to the cow's good character traits. After meeting a few more cows, he began to follow the trend. Then we had to let him in on a family secret we had kept for many years.

Grandpa always chose names for the new cows as they were brought into the herd. With cows, what you see is what you get. Nothing is fake about them. If they are grouchy or having a bad day, you are totally aware of it. Cows don't hold anything back.

Being a people watcher, Grandpa was good at reading personalities. Much like people, cows have very distinct personalities. Some are very laid back, sweet, and easygoing.

Other cows can be mean, grumpy, and jittery. The combination of behavior in the barn and personality traits would determine the cow's name. Grandpa selected cow names from the ladies in the congregation at church.

Reverend Crosley thought naming cows after ladies in the church was a hoot! We told him that was our little secret. He chuckled to himself for the rest of the afternoon. Grandma used to say, "A penny for your thoughts," when she caught me daydreaming. That afternoon, I would have paid a dollar for the pastor's thoughts behind his smile!

Has your family ever kept any little family secrets? Oh, come on, yes, they do! I think all families have inside secrets. Have they ever been exposed in front of the whole church?

While doodling on the bulletin, I heard the preacher mention milking cows during the Sunday-morning sermon. I listened intently as he began sharing thoughts about his afternoon spent in the milk barn with us. The pastor proudly told the congregation about the beautiful black-and-white cow named Barbara.

I spotted my brother a few pews over. He looked at me and rolled his eyes. I then looked toward my grandparents sitting in the middle of the church. Grandpa was smiling and rocking his head back and forth. Fear seemed to sneak into the pit of my stomach, as I knew our little family secret was about to be exposed.

Reverend Crosley continued to tell the congregation about the cow names. He mentioned several ladies in the church who had been honored. I noticed my heart was beating a little faster with anticipation.

The pastor explained that the Teter's cows were named after ladies in the church, and then he began mentioning names. My ears could not believe that the pastor was sharing names. However, he described the glorious honor in such a way as it was sparkly and glamorous. Looking around at my family, they seemed overly relieved.

I was concerned that sharing a name with a big bovine might not be flattering to many women. I watched the ladies whose names had been mentioned as they sat up proudly, smiling brightly while showing honor with no discontent. Then I sat there pondering if the ladies mentioned would ever realize that not all milk cows have charming personalities.

Your perception of yourself can be very different from how others may experience you. Can you relate to that? I sure can. Most of the time, my intentions are far from how I am perceived. I try to be sweet but can come across as prickly.

There is a beautiful rose called the Angel Face. Its petals are an amazing lavender color and have a sweet, fruity smell. However, if you try to pick the rose with your bare hands, the prickles on the stem will quickly change your mind.

Do you have those kinds of days? We all do. Some of us might be smiling on the outside but feeling prickly on the inside.

Some days, you might seem thorny to others. Friend, you are not alone. If you are open to new ideas and listen, God can and will use situations and others to help you grow into something angelic and beautiful (John 10:3–4).

What other people think of you can be one of the greatest fears you struggle with in your mind. God loves you no matter what your friends or family might think (Job 12:4). Just like nature, God always works on you and sees the person He wants you to be. If you do your best at whatever God wants you to do, other people's opinions really don't matter (Psalm 40:8).

Be honest with yourself and ask God to help you examine your heart's motives. Sometimes, it is easy to think you have everything figured out. You know exactly what you should be doing and how to treat others. However, reality and what God thinks can be very different.

We can struggle when we let our minds and emotions get the best of us. Have you been there? Emotions can completely take over a situation.

God's natural process of nature is designed for us to depend on each other and work together. Sometimes, God will use your relationships with others and even nature to help you distinguish His presence and voice, just like He uses you to help others learn about themselves.

Your purpose in life is not a one-and-done kind of thing. You are an integral part of God's creation, created on purpose with many roles. Listen and obey God as He guides you through every intention He has planned for your life (James 1:5). Your ultimate purpose is to have a close, intimate relationship with God.

How you view yourself might differ greatly from how God sees and hears you because He knows your heart. Your heavenly Father is proud of you (Psalm 33:13–15). Listen for God's encouraging voice when you look for His presence, and act when you hear that small voice in your head telling you to get outside and visit your neighbor or help a friend walk their dog. Embracing new opportunities as God guides you will allow you more joy and happiness.

God wants you to trust Him by living in faith and feeling His presence through nature (Psalm 56:3). He didn't create you to live in fear (2 Timothy 1:7). Most of the time, stumbling blocks and anxieties are things we conceive or make up for ourselves to see. Only God will help you recognize the unique situations He has created specifically for you to see.

Maybe it's the pinks and purples you witnessed in the sunrise this morning or the sweet song of a bird singing. Always look for God's presence near you.

God can use nature and animals to help you see and

understand qualities within yourself. We don't always get the answer to our whys. A bad experience can be hard to forget, but good can always come from it.

Sometimes, feelings experienced when you are stressed out can cause an incorrect judgment. One scary experience with a horse might cause you to fear every horse you meet.

Horses are my favorite animals. They are massive yet graceful. If respected and treated properly, they are wonderful pets. My Palomino and Dark Bay horses act more like big dogs. When friends come over to the barn, Bandy and Bop are curious and want to check them out.

People want to get up close and touch the magnificent creatures. For the most part, they are okay with that. When they get tired of people, they walk away. However, not all horses want to be touched by people they have not met. Some horses might not have much patience and bite.

Running up behind a horse unannounced might startle the animal, causing the horse to kick. The horse isn't being mean but reacting with a natural defense mechanism. When a horse is caught off guard, it will jump and react just like you do.

Have you ever seen a horse react when startled? Most animals will respond in the same way.

Horses are big animals, and small things can get in their way. Getting too close or in the path of a horse when walking might cause you to get stepped on. Like all animals, horses must be respected and treated with care so that no one gets hurt.

After working and caring for horses over time, you will learn about their personality and habits by listening to and paying attention to them. Understanding how they function and what makes them tick will change your perception as you gain respect for horses. Fear will change to happiness as you make a new friend, creating an all-new perspective of horses in your mind.

The same is also true of people you meet. The Wikipedia Dictionary defines perspective as "a particular slant or angle for considering an issue, an attitude, approach, or way of thinking." In the big picture, everything you think about starts with your perspective.

How do you try to see and hear people? Why? How you see and hear people and things the way you do forms your perspective. God designed your heart to play a huge role in determining how you view and listen to situations in nature, with other people, and with God.

"Your heart will be where your treasure is" (Matthew 6:21).

The feelings and emotions stored in your heart will either help you see God's presence and hear his voice in nature or block your view. If your heart contains emotions that you have not dealt with and are causing you pain, there won't be much room for love.

Disappointment and lack of trust can cause your heart to lock over time and receive no feelings, not even the beautiful glory of God's love, leaving you feeling like no one loves you because you can't feel love.

Dad always taught me that if I have something to say, then say it. Deal with the issue, get over it, let go, and move on. It means don't bury your feelings down deep or try to just cover them up. Deal with issues you disagree with and settle them. Otherwise, you will be strapped with carrying around unwanted emotional baggage from every relationship.

Wildflowers, a forest of trees, and animals don't hold grudges against one another. Creation needs one another to survive. People need each other as well.

God designed you so that feelings and emotions you encounter from different life situations are stored in your heart.

Feelings of discouragement and disappointment need to be dealt with continually. If an issue is not resolved, it will only build and worsen, causing anxiety. It would be like trying to clean the floor by hiding the swept-up dirt under a rug.

Let's imagine momentarily that you have a beautiful hand-woven rug inside your front door. As guests enter your house, they use the carpet to clean the soil from their shoes before walking into your home. When sweeping the entryway floor every week, you arrange the dirt in a nice pile directly in front of the door. Then you lay the colorful rug over the top of the pile to cover it all up.

After a few weeks, your friends and guests must walk around the large lump hiding under the rug. If you keep this up, your friends might need to use the back door. They won't be able to use the front door because of the overgrown pile blocking the entryway.

You will need to explain what is happening at your front door often. Your friends and family will probably ask why you don't throw away the pile of dirt and eliminate the problem.

Your heart is much like the entryway into your home (Proverbs 27:19). It is the central location for everything you do. It is where your true feelings and emotions hang out.

If you don't clean up the problems that cause negative, bitter emotions, they will completely take over. This will leave no room for happiness, joy, love, and the presence of God to enter and live, forcing everyone you meet to enter through the back door of your emotions instead of the beautifully adorned front door.

There isn't a beautiful woven rug large enough to cover and mask the roots of your heart's problems. The weeds of negative emotions do not just go away on their own; they will grow deep roots in your heart over time (Jeremiah 17:9–10).

If your heart is hardened and locked, it will be evident by

what you say (Matthew 12:34). The thoughts you speak come from the thoughts and emotions stored in your heart (Luke 6:45), which explains why you think as you do.

Bitter people are grouchy and say bitter things (Matthew 15:18–19). They don't listen to others and are focused on their pain. By dealing with your pain and looking at life's challenges for positive factors, you will begin to see situations differently.

Sometimes, a ten-year-old boy doesn't know what to do with his broken heart. After the bus dropped Kevin off at his house, he was informed that his dog Bruce had been shot and buried. The dog had been accused of trying to bite his sister.

His parents did what they thought was best and disposed of the dog while Kevin was at school. To them, it was the end of the story. The problem was solved. Unbeknownst to them, for Kevin, it was only the beginning.

Kevin couldn't discuss his feelings, and no one acknowledged or tried to discuss his thoughts. So naturally, all his broken feelings and disappointment were pushed down and stored in his heart, blocking the entryway for love and trust.

You are not made to carry baggage from the past and try to be happy simultaneously. Your heart needs to see the presence of God every day to help you forgive and be forgiven (Psalm 19:14).

As you open your mind and build a new perspective to see God, look for details and pathways in nature around you to observe God's presence. You will notice that the routine things you consistently do during the day play a big part in determining why you think what you think.

The daily activities, relationships, and places you frequent are essential in building your perspective. A published study in the *European Journal of Social Psychology* concluded, on average, that it takes sixty-six days for a new behavior to become automatic. What are you going to do this week? It's probably the same routine as you had last week.

Many of us tend to walk past nature so often that we no longer notice the simple beauty God created to remind us of Him. You may be sure there are flowers near the sidewalk of your work building, but question yourself when trying to name the color and type of flower. Day after day, you can walk past the same thing many times and no longer see it, forming a habit.

Change your perspective to appreciate the details and fresh smell of the Almighty Creator's art by forming a new habit. Take time to examine the intricate details of nature and recognize God's presence.

Stop to view the beautiful flowers you walk by every day up close.

- Smell the flower.
- Admire the beautiful colors and unique aspects of the flower.
- What shape are the petals?
- Are they shiny or dull?
- Really look at the flower. Notice the design.
- How is it different from the other flowers?
- How is it the same?
- Does the color change when the sun is bright compared to when a cloud blocks the sun?

A new habit can create a fresh perspective, attitude, and frame of mind.

Vision is limited to what your mind and heart allow you to see. You see what you want to see and hear what you want to hear. You know what you are looking for or focusing on with your eyes, heart, and mind.

There is no area of your life untouched by your thoughts

and perspective. You are a creature of your thoughts and habits. You talk to yourself more than anyone else. You are the only one who allows yourself to think and hear things as you do.

"Be a free thinker and don't accept everything you hear as truth. Be critical and evaluate what you believe in" (Aristotle).

Staying open-minded can be challenging. It takes a strong mind not to let other people's thoughts determine how or what you think, especially during troubled times. Immature people are going to criticize. Only you get to decide how you will react.

God designed you to be a part of a community. Considering the views of others is a good thing. Sometimes, words offered by friends and family are true and helpful. But be careful in discerning people's good and bad views (Job 12:2).

Listen to God's voice in your heart for the final decision. Read God's Word, look for His presence in nature, and listen for His guidance.

God is sovereign. Anything that touches your life is allowed by God to fulfill His plan. Disaster can cause you to examine what you believe and how you think much more closely. Even when feeling despair, praise God with every breath you breathe because He gave it to you. God hears your prayers and knows your heart.

In chapter 3 of Job, we see Job agonizing over his troubled situation. Job was probably running all sorts of scenarios through his mind about why everything had been taken from him.

Well-meaning friends come over to visit Job, trying to help their friend by offering him all sorts of advice. Job's friends are confident that a terrible sin caused Job's suffering he must have committed.

After listening to his friends, Job is convinced they are

wrong. "They say, A man's friends should be kind to him when he is in trouble, even if he stops fearing the Almighty? But my brothers cannot be counted on. They are like streams that do not always flow, streams that sometimes run over" (Job 6:14–15). So Job's friends try even harder.

Have you been there? A friend or family member always has a great idea they want you to listen to. Sometimes they are wrong, but other times, they might be right. Many people and situations in life command your attention, trying to pull you away from God's natural presence and voice.

You need others to walk this journey of life with. However, concentrating on their thoughts and not God's can clutter your decision-making process. Opinions should never replace the truth or the facts. Always read God's Word and interact with Him. As Job did, distinguish His presence and voice for yourself in His glorious creation.

What you choose to believe has tremendous power over your life. Listen with your heart and discern the direction God wants you to take with each new sunrise. Be grateful for the opportunity to build your character and confidence while experiencing the awe in every sunset.

Build faith in knowing that you are following God's path for your life.

Getting attached to the outcomes of our thinking and created perceptions is when we stop listening. That still, small God-given voice in your heart provides truthful answers to what you are asking.

"Trust in the Lord with all your heart and lean not on your own understanding; in all your ways submit to him, and he will make your paths straight" (Proverbs 3:5–6).

Faith is built on remembering past God experiences, natural events, and people who have helped form your beliefs. Years of experiencing good and bad situations determine your perspective, controlling how you view and remember certain circumstances.

Life is a journey with God. He has a plan for you day by day. Trust God while you walk together on the journey. Every year, you depend on God for the joy and newness of spring, summer, winter, and fall.

Go outside and appreciate the nearness of the majestic and intricate working parts of God's creations in nature. Feel it in your heart.

Adore the beautiful stars in the night sky as you listen to the crickets singing their night song. Through nature, God will teach, speak, and provide for you mentally and physically. John 1:14 tells us that God intentionally dwells among humans living on earth.

Create a new habit in your life that will bring you closer to God. Instead of asking God why this is happening when challenging situations arise, begin to ask Him how *we* are going to get through this. Listen for and expect that still, small voice in your heart. Pay close attention to what He says.

Changing your perspective while listening to God's positive, wise, and reasonable presence in nature will change your life. That sounds like a lot, but change can happen quickly.

God will sweep your heart clean, removing all fear. Then His spirit can live within, allowing you to do so much more. (Ephesians 3:20). God has a specific plan for you. He's not finished molding your heart yet and never will be.

Points to Ponder

What natural element does God use in the Bible to show himself?

CHAPTER 4

GOD'S PRESENCE
IN AWE

I wanted to help start fires. As I grew older each year, I was allowed more responsibility. While sitting on the tailgate of a pickup one beautiful spring morning, I decided to be more than just a bystander.

Grandpa and Dad had already discussed their plan regarding where to start the fire and how everything would work. There was seemingly no wind that morning, which was perfect. They would drive four-wheelers along the field's boundary, starting and managing the fire. At first, neither was very keen on my fire-starting idea, but finally, they caved and agreed I could help.

Did you ever talk your grandpa and dad into letting you do things that your mom would not let you do? That was so much fun!

Grandpa helped me design my fire starter. We tied three pieces of baling wire together to make one long strand. He looped a couple of red shop rags in and around another piece of wire, making a ball. Then he fastened the red ball on the end of the long wire, completing my "fire-starting" apparatus.

Grandpa dropped me off about a half mile away from the pickup, leaving me with very specific instructions. I was to drag the fire starter behind me along the edge of the field and walk straight back to the pickup. Then I was to sit and wait at the pickup until he returned.

I was thrilled to do my part. Grandpa soaked the red ball on my fire starter with diesel fuel and lit it with flame. I watched him drive away until I could no longer see his red four-wheeler.

Feeling accomplished in my new role, I proudly pranced down the side of the field, dragging my fire-starting apparatus behind me. Dad was lighting fires on the opposite side of the field. I watched the intense flames come to life as the field began to burn.

Can you relate? That feeling of being trusted with more responsibility.

At first, the fires seemed to burn slowly. I quickly calculated when I thought the flames should meet in the middle of the field. By then, I planned to be lounging on the pickup's tailgate, working on my tan.

The warm, sunny day was gorgeous. I could hear the birds singing their morning songs. As I walked, colorful butterflies fluttered near, and cottontail rabbits were eating breakfast. Little did I know I was about to be reminded of the raw power of nature. With a mind of its own, weather can change in an instant.

Within minutes of beginning my perfect morning walk, a massive gust of dust and wind spun around me. I was completely covered with dirt and crop residue. Wiping my eyes so I could see, I watched the whirlwind making its way across the field. Grabbing ahold and twisting the flames, the wind funnel ultimately ignited the stubble over the entire field with fire.

A north wind began to blow, propelling the smoke and

flames toward me. Subject to the blistering heat from the fire burning across the entire field, I dropped my fire initiator and began jogging. Tugging at the neck of my T-shirt, I pulled it up over my nose so I could breathe. The heavy smoke seared my eyes. Trying to run with one eye open, I could barely follow the edge of the field to stay on course.

After what seemed an eternity of jogging, I heard Grandpa yelling through the thick, dark smoke, "Hop on, kid!" I tightly gripped the black metal rack attached to the back of the four-wheeler as we sped down the bumpy field. Grandpa cocked his head sideways and hollered, "Grandma saw the whole thing and isn't happy!" Enough said.

When we returned to the pickup, Grandpa, Dad, and I were covered with black soot and dirt from head to toe. The rubber bottoms of my tennis shoes were melted.

Somehow, Grandma and Mom appeared just in time to witness the event. Let's say they were a little balled up with the situation and leave it at that.

It felt as if nature had played a little trick on us that morning. Even at a young age, I remember being totally in awe of the raw nature of the fire that I witnessed and experienced in the field that day—how the wind completely changed the fire pattern we started in seconds. Maybe God was messing with us just a bit. He does have a sense of humor.

Where have you experienced awe in nature? How have you learned to appreciate the feelings of fear and wonder the "awe" experience can cause?

Being good stewards of the land, farmers and ranchers depend on fire in the springtime to burn pastures and fields. Prescribed burning helps reduce weed seeds and removes leftover stubble and residue from previous crops while reducing the threat of wildfires that can get out of hand.

Intentional burning helps to clear out and eliminate thick

vegetation, safely reducing excess brush and shrubs. This provides an environment that gives new life a chance to come forth, improves wildlife habitat, replenishes the earth, and allows growth.

Yearly burning helps lessen the intensity and reduce wildfire damage while increasing soil nutrients and managing insects and disease. Many states and countries could benefit from this practice.

Fire and many other natural events can trigger or give you the feeling of awe. Awe is a mind-blowing emotion with the power to immerse you in the present moment.

Watching the stunning beauty of a deer running across an open field, jumping over a fence effortlessly with their white tail bouncing, can reconfigure your sense of time. Enjoying the mesmerizing splendor of listening to clear water as it plunges over rocks, continually falling in a cascading descent, provides serenity. Sitting down to relax near the burbling pool of water creates peace for your soul.

God designed awe as an enjoyable emotion for you to experience in nature. The *Greater Good* magazine states, "Awe is the feeling we get in the presence of something vast that challenges our understanding of the world, like looking up at millions of stars in the night sky or marveling at the birth of a child."

While providing a deep sense of fulfillment, the feeling of awe can help to improve your health, gratitude, and self-confidence. Awe will help connect the experience to your creative thinking when focusing on the tiny details of a banana spider's web. Watching a new momma cow lick her baby calf clean can instill goodness in your mind and soul.

Visiting the Grand Canyon was a longtime bucket list item for me. Arriving at the national park, we boarded the tram and headed to the canyon. I vividly remember stepping out toward the edge and viewing the massive natural wonder for the first time. The view is breathtaking, spectacular, and awe-inspiring all at once.

Have you been there? Have you visited the Grand Canyon for yourself?

Nature creates a plethora of ah-ha moments with its breathtaking scenery. The immense feeling of the Grand Canyon, with its beautiful colors and cliffs, made me truly appreciate God's wonderment. The words "This is God" kept running through my mind repeatedly as I looked across the canyon.

I could feel God's presence and wanted to stand there forever, gazing at His amazing creation.

How did you feel looking over the edge? Were you in a state of wonder?

The tour guide informed our group of spectators that lightning was spotted several miles away, and we needed to leave. We were going to be lighting magnets standing high out on the ledge. Quickly piling back into the tram, we left the spectacular view. However, the overwhelming feeling of awe I experienced has never left me. When looking at pictures of the Grand Canyon, I can still sense that God moment I experienced.

Recognizing God's awe in creation promotes the goose bumps you might have felt as you peered out over the rock ledge of the canyon for the first time. "God's voice thunders in wonderful ways; He does great things we cannot understand" (Job 37:5).

You may feel wonder and amazement as you gaze out over God's created beauty in the great outdoors. It can be so overwhelming, enormous, and incredible. This can make you feel humbled and small compared to the beauty you see before you.

"Everybody has seen it; people look at it from far off. God is so great, greater than we can understand" (Job 36:25–26a)!

You might be scared when standing too close to the edge of the Grand Canyon, and you will quickly learn to respect fear by stepping back. Building a connection to something massively larger than yourself creates an emotional foundation for awe while stimulating your strong sense of purpose.

By gaining wisdom from the experience, your heart can seek the correct relationship between your fear and God.

Job was standing on the edge of fear, asking God why. When speaking with Job, God addressed Job's concerns regarding his situation. "Who is this that makes my purpose unclear by saying things that are not true? Be strong like a man! I will ask you questions, and you must answer me" (Job 38:1–3).

God spoke to Job from the whirlwind, not answering any of Job's direct questions because they were not at the heart of the issue. God outlined the correct conclusions and explained His thoughts using examples from His creation.

Can you relate? God doesn't always provide the answer to your why, but He is all-knowing, and you can trust His plan.

The nature God spoke of in His questions to Job is something that, even today, you and I can see anytime, anywhere in the world. You can look up at the sky in Kansas, Hawaii, Spain, Israel, or even Russia and see a beautiful blue sky with white, fluffy clouds.

Anywhere you travel on this earth, you will look at the same sun, moon, stars, and sky that Adam and Eve, Abraham, David, and Jesus enjoyed. How cool is that?

When you allow your heart to soak it all in, you will see so much of God's presence. This will build trust by reminding you of God's power in every fragment of your life.

When you observe nature's majestic and complex elements,

you will realize there is no reason to fear life (Isaiah 43:1b). God is in complete control (Psalm 56:4). Everything belongs to Him because He made it.

The splendor and awe in nature's intricate, finite features prove God is the Creator, highlighting to the world what is important to Him. A caterpillar metamorphosing into a butterfly, speckled robin eggs in a springtime nest, or a delicately spun spiderweb glimmering in the sunlight all highlight God's infinite glory.

Focus on beauty and experience awe. God's handiworks are seen and unseen, yet we depend on them to live life. Everything formed in nature exclaims the awe in God's presence, the Almighty Creator and sustainer of the universe.

Ask yourself questions that focus on God's presence. What aspects of nature you can see, and what are some that you can't see?

God's fingerprint is on the beauty and purpose of every living thing. Through faith, you can see and experience God's heart and presence wherever you look for Him in nature, making you smile.

It's almost like you can't escape the joy in His constant presence when you feel the warm sunshine on your face. I like to think of sunshine as little kisses from God.

Once you experience God in nature, you won't settle for anything less and will smile constantly.

God's awe is reflected in His creation, just as an artist is portrayed in their artwork. Recognizing the characteristics of the painting defines who the painter is—it identifies the creator of the masterpiece.

Vincent Van Gogh was the son of a minister with a Christian upbringing. Vincent loved God deeply and desired to be a pastor.

An article in *Christian Today* explains that after failing the entrance exam to the seminary, Vincent became a missionary to the coal miners in Belgium. A generous man with love for Jesus, he loved others unconditionally. Fired from his missionary job for being overzealous, he returned home.

Vincent struggled with his mental health his entire life. He was a simple man, finally resolving to serve his God through artistic expression. Highlighting the awe in the ordinary beauty surrounding him, Vincent painted his everyday life.

Vincent finally found his calling by painting the natural splendor that God created. Vincent only sold one painting during his lifetime.

In the century after his death, he became one of the most recognized painters ever. His beautiful, world-renowned sunflower portraits were painted to symbolize his gratitude to the God he loved.

Vincent was God gifted with talent. If you step back and take an overall look at his artwork, you will observe the whole story of his painting projects. The subjects of his famous artwork, such as the sunflowers, fabulous stars in the sky, and Bible stories, highlight the awe of nature, created and designed by his God.

Vincent was a painter formed and gifted a unique purpose by a loving God. God can and will use anyone to do anything, including you and your life.

Vincent Van Gogh's life and love for God offer a legacy of individual faith, personal sacrifice, and insightful artistic articulation. Are you allowing God to work in your life? What gifts has God given you to share?

"We must not judge God from this world. It's just a study that didn't come off. It's only a master who could make such a blunder" (Vincent Van Gogh).

Looking back at the overall artistic big picture of creation, you will see God's brush strokes deeply defining His character. Nature is God's story, and He knows His creation intimately.

Everything created and named by God speaks volumes about him, inspiring awe, amazement, and wonder. Sometimes, God's fingerprints are so fresh that you can almost smell the ink.

Distinguishing God's presence for yourself will highlight exactly where He is. Do you see the awe of God's presence in nature? Where?

God is present on earth with us. You can see, feel, and experience His presence in nature every day.

We see God as beginning with nothing. He is the designer of all that is (Genesis 1:1). The complexity of creation shows there is a Creator. God is infinite and beyond your comprehension. Everything God does is for you.

We see God as all-knowing and aware of everything. God understands you completely because He designed you. Nothing is hidden from God. He can hear your thoughts and understands what you wrestle with in your mind. Everything is seen clearly by Him (Hebrews 4:13).

We see God as all-Powerful (Psalm 147:5). God used His power to give man the breath of life. He spoke creation into place, naming the different aspects and performing miracles. God's power raised His Son from the dead. The Almighty Creator does not change and never grows tired or weary (Isaiah 40:28).

We see God as loving. The Almighty Creator is kind, does not anger quickly, and shows mercy, forgiveness, and great love for you and His people (Joel 2:13). His powerful spirit will live in your heart if you ask (Joel 2:12). He designed nature to be glorious while revealing His presence. God is love.

We see God as not hiding. Nature is like God shouting, "Here I am!" He is always right beside you! Our universe details awe in the amazing engineering, revealing our amazing Creator (John 1:3). It is a beautiful reminder that God is ever present and never changes.

God is not a generic kind of God. He is glorious. He is beautiful. He represents artfulness. God loves every artistic thing He designs and crafts.

God creates using color and texture, with many different shapes, patterns, and designs. Many things in nature are distinct yet the same, highlighting unique parts of God's clever characteristics and personality. Feathers are a great example.

If you were to throw a bunch of beautiful blue and green peacock feathers in a pile, each would look precisely the same. An article from BibleTruthPublishers.com explains that all peacocks grow the same patterned "eye of God" feathers.

Every generation of peacocks repeats the same God-designed pattern perfectly because that designates them as peacocks. You could not tell which peacock the feathers came from in that pile of peacock feathers.

After getting to know each peacock that created the feathers, you would realize that each animal's personalities are very different and unique, even though their feathers look the same.

Peacocks are just one example of many things in nature that may look the same yet are unique.

Have you ever watched the amazing colors of a sunset and tried to capture it by taking a picture? The photo doesn't even come close to what you just witnessed, right? That always happens to me.

God generates magnificence so sophisticated that sometimes cameras cannot begin to capture its awe. Standing on a beach ankle deep in white sand overlooking incredible shades of blue waters near the Anguilla shore is a breathtaking, peaceful experience, just one small example of exquisiteness that cannot truly be captured.

After a thunderstorm, you might witness a phenomenal rainbow arching with epic, awe-inspiring colors in the sky. This wonderful vision, which only God can create and is totally responsible for, showcases unexplainable splendor and is a visual reminder of a promise He has made.

Watching astounding beauty and awe that must be seen to believe generates building blocks for your faith, growing your trust in the Almighty Creator and reminding you that seeing is believing.

What gifts of nature do you use daily in life? Ponder that for a moment.

Many forms of artful nature are so intertwined in everyday life that we take them for granted. Fire is a form of nature consistently used, and not just to light candles. We use the heat from a fire to cook supper, warm our homes, provide light, and support manufacturing and refining companies in their daily operations.

The awe of fire is significant to God. He chose fire, a natural element essential to living life, many times in scripture to represent Himself, showing His divine presence (Deuteronomy 4:24). Fire is powerful and mighty. The *Connect Us* editor in chief states that the word *fire* is mentioned 474 times in the Bible.

- The book of Exodus explains how God spoke to Moses from a burning bush, using fire to illuminate His presence (Exodus 3:2).
- Day and night, God used a cloud and pillar of fire to guide the trusting Israelites in the right direction (Exodus 13:21–22). The presence of the one true God

brightly shone before them.

The condition of your heart will determine how you see God and experience the awe of His presence. Everything you do flows from your heart (Proverbs 4:23). Hearts that recognize nature's awe and ordinary beauty will yearn to worship the Almighty Creator, quietly listening to hear His whisper.

God will never turn away from your genuine heart. The more love you have for the Almighty Creator, the more God's love will be provided through the awe in nature you will see. Look with your eyes and feel with your heart.

God already knows what your heart contains, so don't be afraid. Just be honest and ask for His help. Your job is to wait for His reply and let God handle the situation as only He can.

Your heart will determine if you see to believe or if you can believe what you see. Let go of all fear and trust God, allowing Him to guide your actions completely. As a believer, you will see the awe in God's delightful handiwork all around you simply from the love in your heart.

God's heart longs to abide with you in the natural abode He created. Worship the Creator, not His creation (Deuteronomy 4:16–19). Physically, God is not a flower, mountain, bird, or blade of grass. Awe is in the beautiful features God creates, representing his presence on earth and showcasing His heart.

Get outside and experience God's wonder and awe. Nature is a stunning masterpiece that represents God's magnificent presence. When you see God's presence throughout creation, everything else in your life will come into proper perspective.

Ask God to open your eyes and uncover the unique creativity nature incorporates for you to enjoy so that you can see Him. Absorb the awe in nature while intentionally looking for God's presence. Pay attention and be ready to share your new perspective with others. Be more than just a bystander; be a fire starter for God.

Begin writing a bucket list in the back of your God's Presence Diary. List all the beautiful things in nature you desire to see and experience on this fantastic earth you live on.

Today, you will be in awe of God's love and presence in His glorious creation of nature.

Point to Ponder

Who named the magnanimous planet you live on?

CHAPTER 5

GOD SEES AND HEARS YOU

Trusting someone is an earned process that must gather and accumulate over time. Trusting a snake is not on my radar and probably never will be.

Hate is a strong word, and I try not to use it often, but I'm not too fond of snakes. Snakes scare me, and I don't want to be near them. Something about the slithering creatures causes me to dance all over when I am close to one. The farther snakes are from me, the better. Can you relate? Do you have a snake as a pet?

When driving down the road, I automatically lift my feet when seeing a snake. It's not a planned action, just some weird, unconscious reaction. The sight of a slithering snake makes my skin crawl.

I cannot get past thinking snakes are bad, even though I know they do some good things. The snake was cursed when God kicked him out of the garden. He and I are not meant to be friends. However, I admit I have learned valuable lessons from watching a snake.

Loading hay was not one of my favorite chores, but hard

physical work was required to keep the milk cows happy. Dad, Grandpa, and I had our routine down pat.

As a kid, I observed a gigantic black snake while loading bales onto the hay monster one sunny Saturday morning. The snake was slowly working his way up one of the tall wooden corner poles of the hay shed. Its destination seemed to be a bird's nest.

As we continued to load the hay monster, I kept an eye on him. He was so lingering and fat that I thought surely he would not be successful. Gradually, I watched him inch his way to the top. I became acutely alarmed by the baby birds in the nest and stopped working to get Dad's attention. Pausing momentarily, Dad stopped working to hear what I had to say.

I quickly explained to him the ingenious plan I had engineered to save the baby birds. While listening, Dad was leaning on one leg, his hand still holding the hay hook on his hip. His head was tilted to one side, and his eyes stared directly through my skull.

Feeling the odds were already against me, I revealed how "we" could move the hay monster strategically next to the pole. Dad could then crawl up the haystack, knocking the snake off the pole using a hay hook to keep the baby birds safe.

When I was finished, Dad looked at me like I was cracked—shaking his head back and forth, signifying a definite no. He wasn't even remotely interested in my idea. Instead, Dad leaned over and straightened both legs. Standing firm with both hands on his hips, he began preaching another life lesson.

"Deb, that snake represents the circle of life. Not everything in life is good and does not always go as planned. Animals are born, and animals die. The unexpected can always happen. All things happen for a reason. God has a plan for everything. Let nature work its course and leave the snake alone. Now get back to work and move those bales. You are getting behind watching that useless snake."

Can you relate? Have you ever had a great plan, and the person you explained it to just didn't get it?

It was not what I wanted to hear, but I was not surprised. As Dad went back to work, I began a last-ditch effort and decided to try asking God.

While working, I invited God not to let the mean snake eat the baby birds. I would be really sad to watch that happen. If Dad would not participate in my clever plan, God was my only hope for the little birds.

The enormous black serpent reached the top of the shed on his quest to raid the closest feathered nest. Cautiously wrapped around the pole, the snake stretched as far as it could without making contact. Repositioning, it tried repeatedly but could not quite reach the nest.

I watched the sluggish process continue while we finished loading the hay monster. The snake finally gave up and slowly began its descent. His mission failed. I was thrilled!

Hollering at Dad to get his attention again, I pointed toward the snake with my hand holding the hay hook. He looked toward the hay shed, then back at me, and said, "Well, what do you know? Sometimes you win some, and sometimes you lose some. Not everything in life goes the way you planned, Deb."

I nodded my head in agreement. I thought, *True statement, but talking to God seems to help.*

Deep in my heart and soul, I knew God had heard me asking to help the baby birds. God created the giant black serpent and did not allow the hungry snake to eat the sweet babies.

That day, I gained a bucket of trust in the Creator, which began washing away my previous distrust. My tank of faith in

God began to fill, supplying much-needed hydration to the beginning of our new relationship (Matthew 19:26).

What's your story? Where have you seen God work in a way that there is no doubt in your mind it was the presence of God? Jot it down in your God's Presence Diary.

You can trust the nearness of God to help you observe the world differently. Acknowledge His existence.

There are many situations and relationships in life that you won't be able to control. Try shifting your perspective to look for God daily (Matthew 13:15 and Isaiah 6:9–10).

Venture outside to marvel at the authentic big picture, not a puny little view of a made-up world on a screen. God sees you even if you can't see Him (Proverbs 15:3).

Nature is the signature of the one and only God, highlighting His glory. Recognize that you are privileged to live in a universe engineered, created, molded, organized, and administered by the Almighty God (Genesis 21:22b).

God used random, unorganized parts and pieces to create a wholesome masterpiece of beauty. This is an incredible gift to you filled with wonder and designed to inspire.

When I think about the amazing planet we live on, it gives me goose bumps! Every ocean, cedar tree, whale, rock, and human was designed and created by God with a unique function.

Do you ever really ponder that? Everything created was made on purpose, with a purpose, providing a deep sense of belonging. God sees you and chooses you, and you can totally trust Him.

God designed your world by intricately developing each magnificent detail described in the book of Genesis. He is a loving God who created many natural colors to give you a beautiful place to live.

Think about it. God could have made everything black and white, right?

In my mind, there is no way that a bunch of aging monkeys created the Earth or that it randomly exploded into place. However, when God said, "Let there be ..." and it happened, there probably was a big explosion at that point.

God used a sophisticated process with a detailed plan to show you His presence continually. "It is by faith we understand that the whole world was made by God's command, so what we see was made by something that cannot be seen" (Hebrews 11:3). Think about God like there is no box.

"Science is much better at finding things that exist than at ruling out things that don't" (Marcelo Gleiser).

God created nature to provide you with astonishment and enjoyment. Every part of nature works together for you to live life. Creation is authentically God. All of nature sings His praises!

God's immeasurable talent to create and maintain the various life systems making the earth function is repeatedly apparent if you look for them. Can you even begin to imagine how incredibly smart God must be (Job 21:22)?

God created many things you cannot see from your backyard. Solarsystem.NASA.gov explains that the Milky Way Galaxy we live in is just one of over one hundred billion galaxies in the universe. It is comprised of hundreds of billions of stars, gas, and dust, with gravity holding it all together.

God created everything in the galaxy to be connected and to depend upon one another to function.

On a really dark night, Solarsystem.NASA.gov describes the galaxy in which you live as looking like a milky band of light in the sky, thus earning its name. However, you can only take pictures of the Milky Way inside your galaxy.

Unfortunately, you cannot see the entire Milky Way. You live in the suburbs of your galaxy as it measures 100,000 light-years across approximately 600,000 trillion miles.

You cannot look up into the sky and see the process of the Milky Way working. You and I rely on other people with God-given gifts in astrology to explain how the systems in space function around us.

You and I trust that these systems with a God-given purpose work perfectly together.

I heard someone ask why God would create all this space in the universe and only put people on the earth. Isn't that a waste of the universe? I don't know the exact answer because it's a God question, but I have an opinion.

I think the earth is personal for God. He could have filled the universe with other creatures, but He chose to create earth for His people. Earth is the only planet that can support life well. I think God did that to make a point.

We are His people, created with a purpose. God knew you when He formed you in your mother's womb. He knows you personally. God knows the number of hairs on your head and loves you more than you ever realize.

The answer to the question isn't just a head thought or a fact. You need to feel the answer in your heart to understand that you are indeed God's child.

Creation highlights how unique the planet you call home really is. Can you believe you get to live in such a fabulous place?

God designed His colorful creations to show you His love. Once you take the time to look at all the amazing things God created, you might wonder how someone cannot believe that God is the designer and originator.

God designed gravity to be the glue that holds your world

together. You dance with gravity daily.

Spaceplace.NASA.Gov explains gravity as the invisible force that pulls objects toward each other. When you jump into the air or drop something, gravity allows you or the object to land on the ground.

Gravity is God's work. Gravity is His law. You could not live on earth without it. Gravity holds the planets in orbit around the sun and keeps the moon in orbit around the Earth.

The earth is fine-tuned by God and located exactly in the space it needs to be from the sun. God, the intelligent designer, placed the earth in a Goldilocks zone. This allows the planet to maintain a perfect temperature, not too hot or cold. The earth you live on continually rotates on the faultless axes it needs.

In creation, God reminds you that He is in complete control, and you are not fending for yourself. God takes such good care of the earth that you probably don't even realize it. God sees, knows, cares, and always works behind the scenes.

Humans seem to think God created the heavens and the earth, leaving us in charge. Do you ever wonder who ensures the sea has the right saltiness? Have you ever tried maintaining a saltwater fish tank? It is a very meticulous job that I would struggle to accomplish.

The living God did not abandon His creation (Psalm 33:18). He is in charge and maintains it 24/7/365.

In Job chapter 38, God had heard enough from Job's friends. Dismissing God's presence, they took it upon themselves to speak for Him. Trying to decipher the silence, the friends put words in God's mouth.

Assuming God's silence meant He didn't care enough to be present, the ideas and opinions the friends shared missed the heart of the issue. But then we hear God Himself step into the picture and discuss how He created the earth.

God responds to Job by asking rhetorical questions that stimulate awe. We hear God requesting information no human could possibly answer.

"Where were you when I made the earth's foundation? Please tell me if you understand. Who marked off how big it should be? Surely you know! Who stretched a ruler across it? What were the earth's foundations set on, or who put its cornerstone in place while the morning stars sang together, and all the angels shouted with joy?" (Job 38:4–7).

How amazing would that be? I can only imagine God's incredible, strong, confidently booming voice. His intensely smooth expression would make your entire body quiver and the little hairs on the back of your neck stand up when you hear the sound of His overwhelming presence.

"And these are only a small part of God's works. We only hear a small whisper from him. Who could understand God's thundering power?" (Job 26:14).

God asks Job questions that describe aspects only someone who designed and engineered the project would be privy to. Have you ever considered the earth's architectural design and what factors make it function?

I absolutely love hearing about the minute details from the Almighty Creator (Job 38:34–35). "Do you know the laws of the sky and understand their rule over the earth?" (Job 38:33).

God's inquiry to Job was meant to reveal His power and glory. God can do anything and isn't limited to a geographical place, season, or event. Have you ever considered that? Nothing happens by chance, including disaster.

God's supreme power has a controlling influence over your life. The Almighty Creator describes His help.

"When you pass through the waters, I will be with you. When you cross rivers, you will not drown. When you walk through the fire, you will not be burned, nor will the flames hurt you" (Isaiah 43:2).

Nature helps you to recognize that God has absolute authority over all things.

Job replied to God, "I know that you can do all things and that no plan of yours can be ruined" (Job 42:2).

Do you ever fear situations when living everyday life? God has measured everything and is in complete control, sustaining, maintaining, and leading His creation.

What you believe determines what you will do. Friend, you do not need to fear; God's got this.

Doubt and fear are not from God. He cares for you and will speak if you listen. Pay attention and be willing to listen and follow His guidance (Matthew 13:9).

Trust the glory of God's presence in the creation you see before you (Psalm 33:20). Observe God's wonder each day while living without fear. Try not to be anxious about tomorrow or let your cares turn into negative worries (Matthew 6:34).

Trust God's actions even if you don't understand His plan. You can do your part to care for what needs to be done, but ultimately, trust God, who already knows your needs and is your ultimate provider.

God uses His mighty power to design and create the purpose of every natural process on earth so that you can recognize Him. Look out your window, or better yet, go outside and experience nature.

Anywhere in the world, any time of day, you can see, touch, taste, hear, and smell God's presence in nature. When God created, He placed His beauty, glory, and presence in a process around you to experience daily, 24/7/365.

God's presence is available for you to encounter in a bird's song, the leaves rustling on a tree, or the calm wind brushing your face.

The unique details of winter snow, fall leaves, summer grass, and spring flowers unfold with every new season. You can look toward the heavens any time of day and marvel at the process of the beautiful blue sky, the moon, or the stars. God sees you and is always working and creating.

Creation gives you a glimpse of who God is. God perfectly cares for all His creatures harmoniously. His knowledge is inexhaustible. God knows everything about His creation, from surface-level information like your name to the number of hairs on your head. He will never abuse His infinite knowledge.

God designed the earth with nature to nourish and care for you like a mother nurturing her child. Plants, animals, and humans depend on nature to physically heal and survive. Nature doesn't need people, but people need nature.

Our heavenly Father gets credit for creating the universe, not Mother Nature. Scripture says nothing about Mother Nature, yet our society regularly mentions the name.

As defined by *Merriam-Webster Dictionary*, "Mother nature is personified as a woman considered as the source and guiding force of creation." She does not exist and is only a false god. The Bible emphatically states that God made the earth by His power, using His wisdom to build the world (Jeremiah 51:15–16).

The book of Genesis tells us God named the dry land; He "gathered together" Earth (Genesis 1:10). Earth is the only planet not named after Greek mythology.

Earth is an English/German name that means ground or soil. CoolCosmos.com explains that as Greek scientists discovered other planets, they named them after the Greek gods of ancient Roman religion. God designed your world, continues to maintain it, and named it. How cool is that?

Do you wake each morning and test gravity or oxygen to ensure they work correctly? Do you schedule how many times you will inhale and exhale for the day? Of course not. Gravity and oxygen are free and require nothing from you to ensure they function correctly. You only need to think about oxygen if, for some reason, you can't breathe.

Designed to be a fantastic place for you and me to live comfortably, God's earth is the only planet that provides oxygen and gravity. Life begins with your first breath outside the womb and ends with your last breath on earth. You and every living creature require oxygen in your lungs to survive and function.

Gravity, oxygen, temperature, and wind are invisible qualities of nature you can feel but cannot see. Their presence and purpose are essential yet hidden; your eyes cannot focus on them.

God is much like this. You cannot physically see Him, but you feel His presence in the qualities of your heart. God's presence can be felt universally in the love and beauty of creation that encompasses you.

There is no need to try to conceal things from God; just be honest and trust Him. Nothing is unknown from God and never will be. God knows everything about you and loves you anyway.

God intertwined artistic ways to communicate His love for you everywhere in His creation if you relax, leisurely look, and listen (Luke 12:2). Slow down and enjoy what you see.

Lie in the grass and observe. He made many forms of art that are edible, smellable, hearable, touchable, livable, and totally loveable. Go outside, use your God-gifted senses, and experience nature for yourself.

If you are observant, you will see His creative mind woven into the intricate patterns and textures of different rock formations and various geological landscapes. God's passion for color is fully displayed in the clouds surrounding a phenomenal sunset or a field of spectacular wildflowers.

God made every sophisticated detail, color, texture, pattern, and function of creation with a purpose. The unique planet we live on is the only planet with plate tectonics. Geoscience. wise.edu explains that without this process, our planet would look very different, with fewer mountains and volcanos and no deep-sea trenches. God works in ways you cannot understand, but give Him a chance, trust Him, and He will reveal His unique purpose for you.

Nature displays an order that produces trust in counting and organization. The "ordinances of heaven and earth," as mentioned in the book of Jeremiah, are also referred to as "The Laws of Nature" (Jeremiah 33:25–26a). These are factual truths, imminent laws that govern the universe God created.

Laws of nature help to highlight the all-encompassing validation of order that God's nature portrays.

- Pure copper conducts electricity.
- Water freezes at thirty-two degrees Fahrenheit.
- Gravity always rules.

No one completely understands why these things happen as they do. People's opinions about them really don't matter. They occur because God makes them happen.

Nature is far from a snap decision or a randomly large explosion. Creation revolves around God's timing. God calculated nature with a specific plan. He created and named it with great thought so you can trust Him.

God has a master plan and continually works out the meticulous details second by second. Depending upon the weather, creation can provide free energy with sunlight, oil, natural gas, and wind to cool or warm our homes. Earth is designed with distinct details that give you comfort.

God encourages your patience because everything in nature is a process transpiring in His time, not yours. God is sovereign and knows everything. He already knows the result of each process and the exact value it creates within the plan. Everything God does shows His love for you.

I will be the first to raise my hand and say that sometimes I totally underestimate God's power. Some days, I forget how mighty of a God I serve. Honestly, there are days that it is so hard for my frail little mind to remember His strength. I can't wrap my mind around it.

It's as if I limit God because of my thinking and what I can and can't do. Then I seem to put the same parameters on God, limiting what He can and can't do. However, that kind of thinking is not how God's plan works.

God created everything. God is in charge, and I can totally trust Him. God is all-knowing. He's so much bigger and more powerful than you and I can even begin to imagine.

So often, my thoughts and worries about trivial things make me wonder if God can and will fix them. Then I take myself outside in nature to be reminded that God's power made all these colossal gravity and oxygen, the solar system, the sun, and star things. I can trust God with the big things in life.

As I take a long walk and freshly oxygenated air fills my lungs, I think God can care for me because He's got me in His hand. Even though I can't see Him, nature tells me He is right here with me. Yet somehow, this battle with doubt seems to be never ending.

Some days, when fear slithers into my feeble little mind, I struggle to grasp and remember God's presence. However, you and I are assured in God's Word that filling your heart with His presence will never allow doubt or discouragement to win (Romans 12:2).

The condition of your heart and mind is critical to what you believe and how you will handle life situations.

You might pray that God completely removes the mountain or the snake causing the situation. However, the miracle is how God will refine you as He shows you how to walk around the stumbling block.

The ending of one circumstance might be the glorious beginning of something new, providing a new role or task.

Trust God to help you through the trials you are facing. When going through the hard times of life, God is always with you (Isaiah 43:2). God is nearer than you may realize because His spirit dwells within you.

Take the time daily to close your eyes and listen to the wind. Listen to the whisper as it sings, providing music as it slowly sifts through the rattling leaves. Study your surroundings and search for texture, color, and natural beauty.

See and trust in God's presence and be grateful (Psalm 5:3). Thank Him for the beauty He created and named for you to live in (Psalm 33:22). The Creator of the universe shows His glory to provide you with peace.

You may try to make your own plan and shimmy up the pole to the top of your life situation. But if it's not God's plan, be prepared to shimmy right back down the pole to where God wanted you to be in the first place.

Commit to spending time every day looking for awe in nature. Jot down a few words in your God's Presence Diary describing where you witnessed the awe of the Almighty Creator.

Become accustomed to recognizing God's nearness. Talk to Him just like you would a friend. Recognize His glory and get to know Him better (Psalm 27:8).

Observing nature with a fresh perspective can give you a

new attitude and a trusting frame of mind. The best way to resolve your fear is to look for God daily and know He sees and hears you.

God's creation has a rhythm all its own.

Points to Ponder

Do disappointments hold you back from knowing God? Consider how amazing it is that God has a complete plan for the world and your life.

CHAPTER 6

GOD'S WORD IS LIVING AND BREATHING

Our little minds cannot comprehend the magnitude or connectedness of God's plan for nature.

You would be astounded if you could see what God is doing right now. God is probably much nearer than you realize. "He is like a rock; what He does is perfect, and He is always fair. He is a faithful God who does no wrong, who is right" (Deuteronomy 32:4).

Looking for God makes Him easier to see. You can't see the purpose of all that God is doing, but you can see the repetitive fruits of His labor.

God's display of power connected through nature reveals His presence, creating faith and peace. You can see God's presence in the process of nature above, below, besides, and all around you (Deuteronomy 4:39).

The process of how the earth was created is a subject of great debate. Scientists have many theories, ranging from a giant explosion to evolving over billions of years.

While on this earth, you will never know the exact process. However, the Bible explains that one supreme God created the world to show His love (Genesis 1:1–2:3). You might not know exactly how He made it, but you can surely know that God did create the earth.

"Maybe the desire to make something beautiful is the peace of God inside all of us" (Mary Oliver).

Can you imagine if you could have watched God forming the seas and creating dry land? God created with a spoken word (Genesis 1:3).

You would probably be hanging onto the edge of your seat, watching intently as He filled the land with exquisite plants and glorious flowers of all shapes, sizes, and colors.

You would be witnessing the holy moments of God speaking creation into existence (John 1:1–3, Colossians 1:16).

Observing in awe, you would anxiously anticipate God's every move and sound. Clapping your hands with the excitement of a child, you might exclaim, "Do it again, God! Do it again!" (Proverbs 8:30–31).

Yearning to continue in God's presence, feeling like you could never have enough of Him, you would long to witness more holy moments of creation with just you and God.

Filling the earth, we see God's love at work, connecting everything in the process of His plan (1 John 4:7–8).

God creates as an expression of His love, not out of need. God creates with a purpose and a plan and is the author of everything good (Job 36:22).

God created the earth for all creation to live in perfect harmony (Job 34:13–15). The process of nature is repetitively connected from soil to sky, reaching great lengths above and below your feet.

Beginning with a blank canvas, God built the earth one

creation at a time. Encompassing every word He spoke, God constructed a plan by designing with purpose, process, connection, and repetition (Psalm 33:11). Color by color, branch by branch, name by name, God's plan repetitively connected each process with a purpose (Psalm 139:17–18a).

The Almighty Creator crafted and formed with all his heart, displaying good work. Masterminding the entire event, God completed the work Himself. Setting the fatherly example, God labored with a process and manner you and I should follow (Colossians 3:23).

The earth you live on did not just happen. God did not show up late one morning with a big idea, expecting others to accomplish the goal. Hiring someone else was not an option. God engineered the plan, managing and creating the entire project Himself (Proverbs 8:22–23).

You might ask how God's plan affects you. "The Lord himself will go before you. He will be with you, not leave or forget you. Don't be afraid, and don't worry" (Deuteronomy 31:8).

With your best interest in mind, He may not answer your question until the precise time you need to know (Jeremiah 17:10).

God is a loving God (Deuteronomy 5:5). He continually maintains the process of His creation 24-7; you can trust God to take care of you. God never sleeps or slumbers (Psalm 121:3–4). He always knows what is going on even when you don't.

In Genesis chapters 1–11, God describes His foundational plan for creating the earth. God helped humans physically write the words of His story in a book highlighting His presence. The Bible communicates "the good news" and explains things that actually happened.

Scripture was provided to help us understand God's thoughts, ways, and characteristics during good and bad times.

The Bible contains sixty-six connected and related books, all tied together to describe God's story. Reading God's book will present little glimpses of God's identity and provide answers to your questions.

Read your Bible daily to look for God's presence. Ask Him to show you He is real when reading God's book.

Instead of thinking of the Bible as just literature or a book of stories, ask God to show you His presence daily through what you read. God's Word has the same power as when it was written, and His plan will come alive in your heart and mind.

Different aspects of nature are often used as examples in stories and parables within the Bible. God repetitively references the process of His beautiful creation, using something you are familiar with to teach and speak to your heart. Like music, nature is a universal language that surpasses words and speaks directly to the soul (Psalm 19:1–4).

The Bible speaks about the "trees" God named that you see in your yard or on your street (Genesis 1:12). It describes the trees clapping their hands. Look out your window or go outside to investigate their amazing design (Isaiah 55:12).

The light God placed in the sky when He created the earth is still the same sunshine that warms your skin and highlights God's presence today. At nighttime, you and I still look at the same "stars" God named (Genesis 1:18).

The word star means "to burn" or "ash." Job, Elijah, Solomon, and Esther gazed upon the same night sky you do (Amos 5:8). God's plan will continue to endure through all generations. Believe that God is the living word.

God created oceans, mountains, sunshine, tomatoes, alligators, and people. The list of God's creations is endless (Psalm 24:1). Using a process for His plan, God created the magnificent planet on which you live in seven days.

I appreciate this fact, as I am a logical thinker myself. I need a routine to make my life function well. God created the process to show you order, not chaos.

Webster's Dictionary defines the word *process* as "a sequence of actions taken to accomplish a particular plan."

Each specifically designed process in nature's plan piggybacks onto the next, becoming increasingly connected and intertwined with each purpose. Without nature's rhythm, disorder would occur, causing complete chaos.

God created something out of nothing using a step-by-step process that was extremely important in connecting nature's efficiency and purpose. You may not realize it, but everything about life on and around the earth is a processed plan with a purpose.

Every God-engineered process strategically overlaps with the following process, building the cycle in which one purpose repetitively depends on the next to function correctly. Nature's plan is a continual working chain of events. Everything formed and created in our natural living world operates this way.

God designed a fantastic example of this planned process with the little-known dung beetle. This determined insect has the specific purpose of making soil healthy and helping plants to grow.

Cows love snacking on grass and plants. Sun, water, and soil provide a healthy environment for various plants to develop and grow. Eventually, the plant material consumed by the cow will work its way through its body, creating a cow pie. The dung beetle then makes its home in the cow pie.

Immediately, the dung beetle goes to work, changing what the cow left behind into nutrients needed to make soil healthy. The soil can then do its job of creating plants, growing things, and repeating the process. The unwavering dung beetle is a processor of cow poop, making a usable substance for healthy soil.

The dung beetle is just one step in a natural process of steps, with a plan providing clarity and a sense of direction. Nothing happens overnight, and each method requires work and effort. Change can be so beautiful.

God created in order with a plan to provide peace and purpose to your daily life. Planning gives you hope and something to look forward to.

The chaos and upheaval in the world today are not God. Chaos does not serve a purpose or belong in the beautiful world God created.

Plants, animals, and humans all participate in God's creation plan. You have been placed where you are for a reason. You are needed, valued, and exactly where you are meant to be. This can be true even if you are currently unhappy in your situation.

Job was angry, disappointed, and sad, continually telling God all about it. Stomping away mad to sit curled up in a ball, sulking in the corner, shouting, "I'm done with this, just done," was not in Job's nature and would have accomplished nothing. Can you relate?

Job's friend Elihu reminded Job that God could never do wrong (Job 34:10–12). Job's faith in God was far more important than his desire for an explanation for his suffering. "But God saves those who suffer through their suffering; He gets them to listen through their pain" (Job 36:15).

Job continued to talk with God, persistently communicating. Even though he was mad and complained to God in his prayers, he was still praying. He honored God by telling Him his thoughts and feelings.

Have you ever been there? Some days, feelings and emotions can be beautiful pick-me-ups, and others tear you down. But

Job was still talking to God even though his circumstances were terrible. That is the point; God wants you to communicate.

Job was honest with God about his aggravation, feelings, and thoughts. "So, I will not stay quiet; I will speak out in the suffering of my spirit. I will complain because I am so unhappy," Job 7:11 says.

Always feel free to pray and express your opinions to God. This will help you deal with your intense emotions before they get out of hand.

Job was angry with God and complained, but he remained faithful to God's plan. Even though he might have felt that the situation was causing him grief, he remained faithful to God.

Living out your trust in God will help you flourish in His plan and accomplish His purpose for you. Doing what God wants you to do is all that matters.

Disappointment and fear of the unknown can lead you to a pathway of seeing God's grace. Let God direct your desires; that is when God works the best (Job 36:16). Believe that God has a plan for you.

If you are like me, you tend to plan and prepare for how you think your life should go. But how much are you planning and preparing to build God's kingdom? I should ask myself this question every day.

Are you thinking about how your life honors God? What is His plan for your life? These are some tough questions that all of us need to pray about.

Job responded by recognizing that God's ways are best instead of letting his feelings determine his actions.

When you are repetitively discouraged and afraid of how a situation might turn out, remember that our position is to be humble before the holy, incomprehensible God.

God has a purpose and a plan. God is in complete control

of the universe (Job 42:2). Your job is to trust and follow Him (Proverbs 16:3). God watches and sees every step you take (Job 34:21).

If life isn't going quite how you would like it to, and you feel stressed, take a stroll outside to enjoy peace with your Creator. Walking outside in the great outdoors will get your blood flowing. God designed nature to help revitalize your perspective, bringing joy back into your life.

Nature is God's life-processing form of CPR. God's plan for creation is a Process, Connecting God's assigned Purpose of Repeating His love and presence over and over for you to see. Everything in nature is created around PCPR. Trust God's plan.

Process

Nothing about the natural process of life on this earth was designed to be instantaneous. Society teaches us to expect things immediately.

You might want everything at your fingertips right now. However, you will be sorely disappointed if you expect situations, events, relationships, and people to provide what you want immediately.

Life is a process. When God created nature on earth, He lovingly gave you examples to follow. Wildflowers, geese, rivers, and beetles highlight different process qualities we should learn to follow.

Nature is amazing. Nothing in nature is status quo. God designed nature's purpose and process to connect and change constantly.

God promised you, "While the earth remains, seed time and harvest, cold and heat, summer and winter, day and night, shall not cease" (Genesis 8:22). God redecorates the earth four times yearly, and the changing seasons also change your focus.

At the beginning of the calendar year, it is cold and snowy. You focus on wearing coats and lots of layers to keep warm. A few months into the year, the earth begins to wake up into spring, and you can focus on getting outside. Everything is new and beautiful.

As time goes on, the temperature begins to heat up into summer. You might go to the lake, swim in the pool, and spend many hours outside focusing on keeping cool. Soon, the air changes as the leaves on the trees signal autumn is on its way.

Fall leaves provide spectacular red, rust, and golden yellow colors as they dry up, fall off, and disappear with the wind (Ecclesiastes 3:1). Who else could make the end of something so beautiful?

God orchestrates every tiny detail in the process of the earth changing for each season.

Nature is never dull. God designed its purpose and process to connect and change repetitively to fix itself. Nature doesn't need people, but people need nature.

Do you ever thank God for that? Do you even think about or appreciate nature's process? Think how boring and blah living on this earth would be without unique colors, smells, animals, trees, or oceans. God meticulously maintains His creation process daily for you to see and enjoy.

God created the process of nature to share His presence and love with you (1 John 4:8). God is for you and loves you more than you love yourself (Proverbs 8:17).

The Creator wanted to expand His family by inviting you to be His child. God focuses on your heart (2 Chronicles 16:9). His love is unconditional and offered freely, and He wants to live with you (Psalm 25:9).

With each new sunrise, you can explore nature to experience God's heart and feel His joy (Psalm 16:11). If you want to see God, ask Him. Pray that God will show you His loving presence through nature.

God desires you to love Him as much as He loves you. God is all about love, and nothing can separate you from His love (1 John 4:7–8).

The Bible reveals an adoring story about the process of love from our heavenly Father and how it is woven into nature. The heavens will rejoice, the fields will be jubilant, and the forest's trees will sing for joy (Psalm 96:11–12). Genesis to Revelation tells an account of God's love for the people He created.

Scripture is one of the most romantic and passionate love stories ever told and includes nature in many examples. Talk to the earth or the fish in the sea or ask the animals about their Creator. The firstborn of all creation, Jesus, created and is the visible expression of the invisible God of love (Colossians 1:18).

Focus on God's love to help you restore your perspective and belief (1 John 5:5). You cannot control or determine the process or path of love, as it is a force of nature with a mind of its own. Love has no boundaries or limits (1 Corinthians 4–7). The Bible states that even water cannot quench love, and rivers will not wash it away (Song of Solomon 8:7).

You can learn to see God with different eyes and allow Him to use you in His process. Let love be your legacy. If you will let Him, Jesus's love is designed to fill the hidden places and deep cracks in your heart. Simply ask God to fill your heart with His love.

People will remember how you made them feel and will be affected by your beliefs. Love is a process of connecting with others. Continue passing your story of God's love to the next generation so it does not end with you.

Connection

Life is a precious process that connects you with others and nature, fulfilling God's purpose and plan. Your purpose directly connects you to God's natural process.

Have you ever seen the writing on a headstone in a cemetery? The line after the name generally lists the dates the person was born and died, creating the dash between the dates from birth to when we leave this earth.

Our life on this earth is summed up in one little dash. We strive to accomplish and connect as much as possible during the one precious "life dash" we are gifted.

When you leave this earth, people will remember how you made them feel and the connection you have with them. Physical things will not matter. You are not taking those new boots, the business you built from the ground up, or the plaques and trophies you have earned with you.

Things gathered in life are unimportant; the seeds of love you scatter will define you. What matters most is spreading those precious seeds to connect with people.

God's presence is in the community. Trees, goats, bees, and you are all designed to connect with others fulfilling a purpose, helping others provides you with a sense of self-worth.

Isolation and loneliness can make you feel like you have no purpose. Friendships and relationships are built by living in the same hive, walking in the same pasture path, and assembling your stories.

We seem to get so caught up in our own little world, focusing on our presence and what we see on the screen in our hands, that we forget to look at what or who is sitting next to us.

Set down your screen and look around at who and what surrounds you. It is tough to notice the beautiful blue sky above without actually looking up.

Social media is funny, right? It was designed to connect and bring people together, but instead, it has created a world of its own. Living life through our screens establishes an atmosphere of recognition without connection. Allowing fake friends makes it okay to pretend and escape reality.

God has gifted you and me with talents that let our stories and creations speak for themselves. Even though their name is not visible, it is obvious who created the sunflower masterpiece.

Reading their poetic words, hearing their phenomenal voices, or seeing their artistic creation causes you to connect and feel like you know them. Even though you have never met, you might consider them a friend.

Michelangelo's *David* has become one of the most recognized works of Renaissance sculpture. Looking at the fine details, those with a trained eye automatically acknowledge the talent of the God-gifted artist.

The seventeen-foot statue reminds us of David, the man after God's own heart. The biblical icon symbolizes strength and youthful beauty. Michelangelo was a believer endowed by God, serving with his artistic talent.

God's name is well-known and recognizable worldwide. Sadly, some people can hardly speak without using the name of God and Jesus disrespectfully in their vocabulary or texts many times every day.

God's works of creation connect and speak for themselves. God is the real deal; there is nothing fake about Him. People don't define who God is; God defines who people are.

Nature tells God's unique connection story. Highlighting the splendor and characteristics of who God is in the masterpiece He created. We don't need to see God's name stamped on the bark of a tree trunk or embroidered on the backside of a giraffe to believe that He is the Almighty Creator and designer.

Nature speaks for itself while providing a connection to the feelings of comfort and safety. Connecting beautiful signs of His wondrous love right before your eyes. There is no need to worry or fear about living life. You are submerged in God's creation 24-7. It is apparent only if you choose to look.

You can learn, explore, and focus on your connections to creation, others, and God. Let your relationships affect and shape your life as they are naturally designed to do.

You must be a friend for you to have a friend. Connect with God and people. A few connection possibilities are listed below, but the possibilities are endless.

- Locate a church near you and get involved.
- Search for local community groups and find people with the same outdoor hobbies as you.
- Get to know your family better by taking a walk together.
- Make friends with people you work with.
- Meet your neighbors, invite them over for a meal, or go outside and play frisbee.
- Smile and talk to the people you are waiting with at the store.
- Go to the lake, go hiking, fish, or catch some rays.

Connecting with nature and others will add value to your life.

Purpose

God has a plan for everything. God put you right where you are for a reason, and you are chosen. He designed you with many gifts and talents. You are created on purpose, for a purpose.

Everything has a purpose, a unique place, and a reserved seat on this earth. Essentially, we are all floating in the same boat and can relate to one another. Beginning with the same story, you and I are here on purpose.

God created a script for your story long before you were born. You are a part of God's plan that outlines His story. Uniquely knitted in your mother's womb, you developed until birth. At birth, your distinct purpose begins. In God's designed plan, you connect and intertwine with other people and create things in God's designed role.

Why are you on this earth? Look through the lens of God's plan. Your designed purpose is what God wants you to do, not what you think you should do. God has a plan for your life that is way better than yours will ever be. God made you to love Him and others.

God assigned everyone with talents and gifts that contribute to their role and are part of the plan. No one else can take your place. Even identical twins do not wear the same fingerprint; each is unique. Every zebra, rock, rain cloud, galaxy, human, and pine tree embraces something special.

God can use anyone to do anything. Sometimes, your purpose may change depending on the season and circumstances life throws your way.

You are created with a unique personality and a brain to think—a heart to feel love and a mouth to enjoy laughing and smiling. You are blessed with feelings and emotions. Every created being is fashioned with a purpose.

There is no need to stress over finding your purpose. Don't worry about it. God will guide you and send you in the direction He wants you to go.

Talk to God out loud and ask Him what He wants you to do. If you live as God wants, your purpose will find you.

Life is not easy; you will always have challenges, and sometimes things don't make sense. Some days, you might feel like you are constantly driving fast over steep hills, hanging on for dear life as your emotions move repetitively up and down. Yet you might feel peaceful other times, like silently floating in a kayak on the water, smooth as glass. Strive to live life to its fullest, following God's plan day by day.

Size doesn't matter when it comes to purpose. The hummingbird's job is just as crucial as the elephant's. Both are beautiful and wonderfully made.

God intentionally creates the big and the small, carefully defining the minute details. God made mountains and oceans, yet He knows the ladybug and puts life into tiny seeds. Assigning each a critical job, God loves His creations perfectly.

Sometimes, I wonder about all the tiny babies that are aborted each day. We seem to live in a self-centered society that promotes the slaughter of unborn children because they are an inconvenient consequence of people's irresponsible actions. Each of those babies was designed and created with a unique purpose and a special gift.

What blessings is the world we live in missing out on because these babies cannot use their gifts to fulfill their purpose? One of them may have been the next Michelangelo, Einstein, or gifted scientist to create a cure for all cancers. These are tiny wonders that this earth has been denied, and we will never know their purpose.

Thankfully, many years ago, a young, unwed woman chose not to abort her baby. She allowed her child to fulfill the process of God's purpose. Mary listened when God told her to name her baby Jesus.

Your purpose is a lifelong journey that changes over time and never ends. It is not a one-and-done thing neatly tied up in a box. Instead, recognize it as a continual step-by-step process, beginning at birth and not ending until you leave this earth.

God will place you daily in situations to help others. Your responsibility is to choose how you respond.

Repetition

God designed everything in nature with a purpose and important reason to exist, including the beautiful patterns you see and enjoy.

Early Greek philosophers studied nature's diverse shapes, patterns, and designs, trying to explain efficiency and order. Mathematics, physics, and chemistry are distinctly seen in nature. They aim to seek, discover, and explain patterns and regularities of all kinds at different levels.

With only a glance, God designed your eyes to distinguish repeating shapes. Schools of fish, a forest of trees, and ripples created by wind moving loose sand are all examples of repetition in nature. As your brain recognizes only one of the shapes, it automatically knows the rest are identical.

God incorporated repetition into the fantastic, planned environment you are blessed to live in. He designed nature using distinct reoccurring patterns, rhythms, and shapes you can recognize, which provide order and help you remember and believe.

Visual natural patterns are explained in chaos theory, topology, and many other mathematical patterns. Science World explains that mathematics is sometimes called the "science of patterns."

Strikes of lightning, the branching of blood vessels, and leaves on fern plants are infinitely self-similar, demonstrating the fractal pattern.

Your right hand looks the same as your left hand. Visual patterns or symmetry look the same on both sides, explains kids.kiddle.com. Many species of animals have symmetrical patterns.

Tigers are relatively symmetrical down the right and left sides, beginning from the midline of their body. The stripes on the right side of a tiger's face look the same as on the left.

Spirals are curved patterns that focus on the center point. They are common in plants and some animals. Pine cones, pineapples, seashells, and hurricanes are all examples of the spiral pattern you can see.

Nature repeats things for your benefit. Knowing what is coming up next helps you to feel more comfortable.

One ear of corn always looks identical to the next ear of corn. When you pull down the shuck, your mind expects what it will look like. Many kernels all lined up into perfect, even-numbered rows. Repetition soothes your brain.

However, variation is possible in natural repetition. Diseases and insects can alter the formation of any pattern, causing changes to the color or shape of the rowed kernels.

Despite the slight variations, the ear of corn still meets the picture of your mind's expectation. Isn't it amazing how God provides you peace of mind in the simple, dependable source of repetition, such as yummy corn on the cob?

The skin of a giraffe, corn on the cob, a honeycomb, or a head of garlic all demonstrate the efficiency of the Voronoi pattern. The laws of physics apply mathematics to God's world of nature perfectly.

"The Book of Nature was written in the language of mathematics" (Galileo Galilei).

Nature repeats God's love over and over again. The repetition of something good or something you depend on seeing earns trust and builds hope. Can you relate?

Trust doesn't occur overnight; it requires precious time to accumulate. Learning to live and trust in God's presence in the nature you see daily builds faith and belief in God, providing joy and peace deep in your heart and soul.

There is beauty in repetition that provides consistency and relationship. Doing the same thing over and over again creates a sense of stability.

What are you going to do next month? Probably pretty much the same thing you did last month. You and I are people of habit and repetition, designed for happiness that comes from routine.

It would be best to have guidance to focus your thoughts and life on truth. "Fear not," the most repeated command in the Bible, is repeated at least 365 times.

Basically, God is telling you over and over every day not to be afraid. God provides order; society creates chaos. Repeatedly saturating your mind with God's Word will keep His promises in your heart.

The Bible consistently repeats themes and ideas. In Philippians 3:1, Paul explains that he doesn't mind repeatedly writing the same things to help people be ready.

We are forgetful people. God's Word will repeatedly remind you of His promises, explaining what He has done and will continue to do to encourage you to believe in Him.

What things do you like to read? Choose what you read and follow wisely; there is no need to live in fear.

Summary

Everything in nature is a life-regenerating process created around PCPR. Creation is the Process, Connecting its Purpose of Repeating God's love and presence over and over.

Nature doesn't need humans, but humans need nature to survive. God created nature on earth as one complete system that works within itself (Revelation 4:11). God engineered, designed, and created with a detailed plan.

Nature is an excellent example of how faithful God is. Can you see His story daily in creation?

God Himself is always with you and will never leave you alone. You can feel God's love in the sunshine, warming your heart and face as your faith and trust in the Almighty Creator grows. God's story of nature shows that He is the only one you can totally trust.

In the next few chapters, you and I will walk through nature and look for God's presence. God's ordered process and purpose will be revealed to help you see and understand the beauty in His natural designs.

You will see how the lifesaving aspects of PCPR weave into every aspect of nature and your daily life. Nature encompasses so many different things. Through nature's secrets, you will begin to understand and recognize your many connections with God (Matthew 13:16).

God speaks visually through creation and verbally through the Bible. As you read this book, focus on the creation around you, listening for God's voice to distinguish direction.

Silence is a part of nature. Allow the process and glory of nature to sink into your soul. Slowing down doesn't necessarily describe your speed. Learn to be still and listen for God's direction (Exodus 14:14).

Nature is God's life-processing form of CPR. You will see the presence of God for yourself in creation through PCPR, viewing the possibilities of a world you have lived in but may have never considered.

Once you see God's artful design in nature throughout your day, you will never unsee it. God loves you, and thankfully, His passion happens to be saving lives. You can trust God's plan.

Points to Ponder

What is one process in nature radiating God's love that repeats daily, highlighting that He is entirely trustworthy?

CHAPTER 7

GOD DEFINES EACH DAY

*D*oesn't the thought of a gorgeous blue sky with puffy white clouds warm your heart and make you smile?

I bet you are smiling right now just thinking about it! Each day, the Lord has created just for you (Psalm 118:24).

The first chapter of Genesis describes how God lovingly created light. The first creation made by God's word separated the light from the dark. God named the light day. At the beginning of every new day, darkness becomes light. Time began with the first sequence of day and night.

After creating plants, God, with His great power, spoke the brightness process of the heavenly lights into place. He placed two large lights in the sky to shine repetitively and regulate the light on the earth. God made the brighter light to rule the day. The lights determine signs, seasons, weather, days, and years (Matthew 16:2).

God delivers a spectacular sunrise alarm clock each morning for you (Job 38:14). The golden sun ascents while pursuing a calculated path into the infinite blue sky, escorting you through your day. Progressing slowly, the big orange ball's course provides you with time, warmth, and a schedule (Psalm

136:8). God's glory and wonderment are in the natural light He creates (Psalm 36:9).

God is light with no darkness at all. God's presence shines on a clear, bright, sunny day when you look up to the heavens. It's like God is saying, "Hey, here I am, have a great day! I've got you in my hands. If you need anything, just ask" (Psalm 89:2).

God is personally thinking of you by name today as He provided the clouds as a possible form of entertainment (Job 37:16). If you have time on your hands, lay on a blanket and look up at the sky.

Study clouds' shapes to see what kind of animals or any other shape you can imagine from looking at them. Share this activity with your kids or kids at heart.

I have always been an early riser and blame it on the farm girl thing. As a young girl, I eagerly assessed the morning clouds when my eyes were open. Peering out the east window of our second-story, hundred-year-old farmhouse, I would anticipate the possibility of a fantastic sunrise, hoping for the kind of color display only the heart of God can create.

On the days when the weather cooperated, I adjusted my pillow for an optimum view, admiring the spectacular show in complete comfort. Pinks, lavenders, yellows, and orange hues exploded in the Kansas sky just before the sun popped above the horizon. It was as if God was saying, "Good morning, Deb! I've got this day. Have a fantastic one!"

Can you relate? Do you love to watch the sun rise?

Has there ever been a day when the sun has slept in or not risen to do its job? Some days, clouds may cover the sun, but do you question if the sun is still in the sky? Of course not. You can still recognize the sun's natural light. Each new day begins with a glorious sunrise, a blessing, a fresh start, and a new chance to begin again.

"Today is the first day of the rest of your life." This quote is from Charles Dederich, a reformed alcoholic attempting to help anyone with any addiction. Today will be great when you realize how wonderful it is to live in the present and not yearn for the past or future.

No two days are the same. Each day is distinct and unique, and it is worth enjoying. Every morning, intentionally consider each new day. This will affect your head and your heart.

- This is a new day, and God has blessed me to live on this earth.
- This is a new day to watch the fantastic sunrise and see God's presence in nature.
- This is a new day to bless my neighbors and take them flowers.
- This is a new day to show my kids or grandkids how to love others.
- This is a new day that I have been blessed by relationships with friends and family.

How you live out each new day matters. Do you believe in what God can and will help you do?

God hung the heavenly lights in the sky to show you His love when creating. Every morning, the sun showcases God's splendor in the blazing sunrise. The power in God's hands is like the rays of light that radiate from the sun (Habakkuk 3:4).

During the day, you can see the same big orange ball of sunshine anywhere on earth. This is a continuous reminder not to be afraid. Can you trust that God's presence is always nearby and will never leave you?

God is constantly taking care of you and me, 24/7/365. God created nature with the specific purpose of working in tandem to provide everything you need. Things like food, healthier bodies, better sleep, and beautiful colors are all a part of nature.

As the sun rises in the east, it eliminates the darkness of the night. Warming the earth creates an atmosphere for God's plants, animals, and people to thrive.

Photosynthesis is a process that influences plant growth and drives the ecosystem. The most critical variable is changing the sunlight into chemical energy, growing plants that make food for you and me.

Light affects plants, but animals and your body also benefit from sunlight. God designed your body to absorb the sun. Eposts.com describes how sunshine stimulates animals and produces vitamin D, increasing calcium absorption to strengthen bones and reduce osteoporosis.

Do you have problems sleeping? God provided sunshine to help with that as well. According to sleepfoundation.org, the sun can help you rest. This is accomplished by improving circadian rhythms, an essential God-given twenty-four-hour cycle that is part of your body's internal clock process.

Light is the most potent influence on circadian rhythms. The sun helps your body produce more serotonin, improving your sleep-wake cycle.

On a sunshiny day, when you walk outside, can't you feel your mood improve? It has been proven that sun exposure can make you happier and help you to relieve stress. That's because God invented your body to react to sunshine.

Healthline.com shares that sun exposure increases serotonin levels, giving you a more positive perspective. Sunlight triggers special areas in the retina of your eye, initiating the release of serotonin. Naturally, increasing serotonin will boost your mood and help you to focus.

You have God-given feelings and emotions that directly connect you with nature. How cool is that? Get outside, smell the flowers, and feel the warmth on your skin from the sun high up in the sky. Be happy, enjoy the day, smile, and share the brightness of your smile with others.

God strategically used sunlight to provide a mixture of colors you can see. Sciencelearn.org shares that your eyes would not see the color without light. Wavelengths of light form light, and each wavelength is a specific color. The color of an item you see is from the wavelength of light that is reflected in your eyes.

Color can affect your overall mood and how you experience the world around you, explains WebMD.com. Colors can affect you by suggesting certain emotions and feelings. You can use color to send a message or meaning simply by the color of your clothes.

Gazing at the splendor of nature tells us that God obviously loves crafting and initiating many colors with His light. I think God created color to awaken and strengthen our belief in Him.

Ponder your natural surroundings for a minute. Anywhere in the world, if you look up on a clear, sunny day, the God-designed sky is a gorgeous shade of blue.

If you are fortunate enough to be near one, God designed transparent bodies of water to look blue. Artsy.net explains that most blue objects are consistently positive, and very few are associated with opposing ideas.

"Blue is a soothing color, promoting clear communication," states SparkGrowth.com. The internet and many social media platforms use blue, as it is recognized with words such as calm, logic, and royalty.

An article by Alex Loana on Medium.com states, "Americans overwhelmingly prefer seeing paintings of outdoor scenes, 88 percent to 5 percent for indoors. We are partial to observing subjects such as lakes, rivers, the ocean, 49 percent, and forests 19 percent—namely, shades of blue and green." Pictures of trees, flowers, and water scenes are prominently used in hotels, hospitals, and medical offices to promote tranquility.

International Lifestyle magazine revealed from a worldwide survey that blue is the most popular color in ten countries across four continents, including China. Green is the second most popular color in Thailand, China, and the United States.

I must admit that every time I see a fabulous blue sky shining over lush green grass, I smile and think of Grandma and the question she asked that changed my perspective of God forever. She was full of wisdom. Maybe Grandma was right about blue and green being God's favorite colors.

What do you think of the colors blue and green? How do they make you feel?

God created humans in His likeness (Genesis 1:26), so it's no wonder most people favor blue and green colors.

I love that our Father God shared His artistic passion for colors with you and me when we were created. I adore seeing all the different colors of flower petals, shades of blue in the ocean, and various color patterns of animals that remind us of His presence.

One of the most brilliant displays of light and color is the rainbow. Rainbows provide beauty you cannot touch but can only see with your eyes. God created the rainbow to be almost an optical illusion coming out of the clouds fashioned into a glorious arc of color.

Kidsplayandcreate.com explains that the rainbow appears in reflection and refraction, the bending of sunlight in raindrops. The rainbow is a full circle.

Standing on the ground, we see one arch because we can only see the light reflecting off raindrops that appear above the horizon. Sometimes, people on an aircraft can see the full-circle rainbow.

God told Noah, "The rainbow is a sign of the agreement that I made with all living things on earth" (Genesis 9:17).

In an article in *Urban Well* magazine, Josh Elsom explains

that no Hebrew word for rainbow exists. The word translated is the same word used as archer's bow.

When God created the rainbow, He hung His warrior's bow in the clouds as a pledge. The rainbow reminds God Himself that He will no longer use flooding rains as a resource of judgment (Genesis 9:11–16). Peace in the rainbow is found in understanding God's promise that rain will never be used against all living creatures again.

Have you ever been fortunate enough to see the full circle of a rainbow? I haven't, but it is on my bucket list.

Have you ever seen an Etch-o-sketch? You might have played with one as a child. Turning the knobs on the lower front makes the little cursor draw a picture. Kids love to draw pictures of the things they see outdoors.

I have always needed more patience or talent to design a flower or tree picture on an Etch-o-sketch. I was content with drawing lines all over the screen.

The best thing about the toy was that it didn't matter what you did on the screen. Pick it up, shake it, and get a completely new screen. A do-over anytime you want!

God provides you with a do-over every morning the sun comes up. It doesn't matter what happened or what you did the day before. He still loves you.

God turns your darkness into light, providing you with peace and joy. Each new day is a trustworthy promise instilling living hope in your heart.

Even with a magnificent sunrise, sometimes the process of your day doesn't go well. Right? I have had days when I felt like I might be better off returning to bed and starting the whole day over. Ever had one of those?

The book of Job explains that Job was so miserable in his situation that he cried out cursing the day he was born. "Let that day turn to darkness. Don't let God care about it. Don't let the light shine on it" (Job 3:4).

Sometimes, your day might end entirely differently from when it first started. Maybe your good friend put you on red after a disagreement, you rear-ended the car in front of you at a stoplight, or your uncle was killed that day in a farming accident.

Never underestimate how vulnerable you may be when stuck in discouragement or times of hardship. Fear takes over when you struggle emotionally, physically, or spiritually.

Hold on to God's light even when relief seems to be nowhere in sight (Isaiah 44:8). God will never abandon you. Trust God and draw your strength from His presence.

Jesus completed miracles of healing the sick, feeding thousands of people, and bringing people back from the dead, yet the Pharisees still did not believe. Sadly, miracles will never convince those who are only skeptical.

Faith and belief will help you to see the miracles God designs daily in nature. We are all part of nature. Recognize the light of God's blessings only He can create on earth through nature and in your life.

Do you connect and know that God defines each of your days with a miraculous production of color that emphasizes and connects you to His presence? He wakes you with a glorious sunrise every morning and ends the day with a fantastic sunset. God repeats the process of light every twenty-four hours in His plan.

Throughout the day, you can physically watch the miraculous purpose of the sun as it slowly slides across the sky. When you feel the warm sun on your face, know it is a kiss from God, who never sleeps. He sees you and walks through the process of each day with you.

Thank God for His presence as you see the sun streaming

golden light through the trees and the beautiful blue sky shining above you. The best way to improve your day is to pause, stop whatever you are doing, and thank God for being there with you. True silence is rare; that includes even making your mind silent.

God knows when you have had a bad day. He wants to connect and help you deal with the struggle of trying to understand why you didn't receive the happy ending you had hoped for.

Nothing surprises Him. God is not hiding (Psalm 22:24). He desires to connect with you and have a relationship with you.

When the sun drops below the horizon, it is time to wrap up the day, put on your jammies, and rest. Repeating the feeling of awe, marvel, and amazement each day as you see the sun strengthens your faith in God's process, building living hope (Matthew 5:16).

God placed lights in the heavens so that people could see and connect to His presence no matter what town, state, or country they were in.

After hours of resting in nighttime darkness, God brings the light of a new day, allowing you to choose what you make of it. Just because a situation happened yesterday or maybe last week doesn't mean it will happen again.

Regardless of what has happened in the past, allow yourself to let the baggage of yesterday go and be happy in the presence of a new day. What you believe will ignite and stimulate your thoughts and create vision.

God knows your name, so live like it. Every day is a new start. God's Word brings the light of a new day to life (Psalm 119:105). From dawn to dusk, continually praise God in all His glory. (Psalm 113:3).

CHAPTER 8

INTIMATE REST

*A*s the sun sets in the west, darkness overcomes the earth (Psalm 136:9). The absence of natural light directs you into nightly slumber to rest.

Genesis chapter 1 describes how God strategically created the dark, naming the darkness "night" (Genesis 1:5), forever separating light from dark on the planet we call home (Psalm 139:11–12).

While traveling to pick up online farm auction treasures, my farmer husband and I stumbled upon the Cave of the Mounds in Wisconsin. The cave is made of natural limestone. It was discovered accidentally by a farmer working in one of his fields. We took a guided tour of the cave to witness all the fabulous, colorful crystals formed by various minerals.

As we walked through the cave, the tour guide would turn on the lights ahead of us. At one point, the guide gathered our group to explain the capabilities of the immense darkness the cave commands.

She explained that the complete absence of light, or true darkness, is a natural phenomenon not manufactured by humans. It occurs only in two places on earth: a cave and the bottom of the ocean.

Our guide instructed the group to stand in a circle as she turned the lights off, demonstrating the depth of darkness in the cave. She explained that you are now basically blind, and your eyes require light to see.

Standing in the dark cave, I tried waving my hand in front of my face. No matter how close my hand was to my eyes, I could not see a thing.

The toddler in our group became uneasy very quickly and did not want to play the game for long. As the lights came back on, my eyes rapidly readjusted to the light.

I am so thankful that God provides ways for you and me to see. Can I get an amen?

Ever since God created you, your days have repeated the nighttime cycle. As darkness begins, you know it is time to finish your day, rest, and relax.

At night, the beautiful moon is visible in the sky, fulfilling its purpose of illuminating the earth (Genesis 1:17). Created to rule the night, the moon also provides the earth with signs, seasons, days, and years (Genesis 1:14). The moon and billions of stars shine, lighting the sky as everything on earth sleeps.

Have you ever noticed that the moon affects your sleep? SleepFoundation.com found that the full moon was associated with less sleep and lower quality sleep for those who participated in a sleep study.

During the full moon, participants experienced longer times to fall asleep, less sleep, and a 30 percent reduction in REM sleep. Intensities of light are one of the most significant influences for falling asleep and how well you sleep.

God designed the moon to be the most significant light in the night sky. The moon provides light to see at night, reflecting the sun's light on Earth. Solorsystem.nasa.gov compares the size of the moon to Earth. If the moon were the size of a pea, Earth would look the size of a nickel.

Trueorigin.org shares that the Earth and the moon are created to be tidally locked. This means that the moon rotates at exactly the same time as it takes to orbit the Earth. This explains why the same side of the moon is always turned toward the Earth. God created the moon to help stabilize the Earth's climate.

If you could visit anywhere in the universe, where would it be? The moon is the only location outside of Earth that humans have visited.

Earth appears as a bright blue and white object from the moon in the black sky. When I see the moon visible during the daytime, it always reminds me of God's presence, as if He is smiling down on me. He is constantly watching over you and me day and night.

God placed bright stars in the night sky as the moon's companions. "The sky was made at the Lord's command. By the breath from His mouth, He made all the stars" (Psalm 33:6).

Anywhere in the world, at any time of night, you can witness God's design for the moon and stars, creating a great canopy of lights that shine brightly in the peaceful heavens. Their glorious twinkle and shine give you a feeling of security and stillness to help you rest in the darkness of the night as God's glory shines.

Did your class ever visit a planetarium at a young age to learn the story of stars?

In grade school, the annual field trip to the planetarium was the highlight of the school year for me. With great excitement, my classmates and I would comfortably lean back in the chairs of the dark, cool room.

The domed ceiling would seemingly come alive with replicas of the bright stars in the night sky. We followed the narrator's red guiding light on the ceiling with our eyes as it pinpointed the bright stars outlining constellations.

Trying to memorize the location of as many constellations as possible, I was eager to go home and stargaze at the night sky above our farm. Sharing my new knowledge at home with family was exciting.

I convinced them to go outside in the dark so that I could proudly point out the constellations I had learned that day. The darkness of night compels you to see the fantastic, star-filled sky above your head.

God hung the stars by articulating their assigned location. The system in which stars function epitomizes God's incredible order and effectiveness. Some scientists suggest that the number of stars in the sky equals all the grains of sand on earth (Psalm 147:4).

Job is considered one of the oldest books in the Bible, written approximately 3,500 years ago. The Bible explains that when God asked Job questions, He referred to specific star constellations. God explicitly mentions the constellations Pleiades, the Bear with its cubs, and Orien's belt (Job 38:31–32).

I find it fascinating that the stars Job looked at are the same constellations available for you and me to look at in the night sky even today.

Over one hundred billion stars live in our galaxy, according to Cs4fn.org. Each one is just as unique as you are. Each star owns its exceptional brightness, color, and sound. Stars sing memorable songs generated by their size.

Much like musical instruments, more prominent stars have a deeper sound. Smaller stars sing at a higher pitch formed from actions inside the star. God designed each star to have its unique way of making a joyful noise (1 Corinthians 15:41).

The US Navy has returned to the basics of teaching young officers to navigate by looking up to the heavens. NPR.org explains that relying only on GPS can cause many problems if GPS satellites are jammed, hacked, or destroyed.

Sailors traveling across the open ocean without landmarks can use the stars, moon, sun, and horizon to calculate their location. Stars have an essential purpose for navigation and direction. The navy is teaching the new officers to use their perceptiveness to follow nature.

When you study the aspects of nature, does it become more evident that there is a definite plan and design? The minute order of details, the intertwined processes all over the earth, and the timing of everything in nature are astounding.

I think believing the world exploded into place or evolved on its own takes way more faith than believing God is the Almighty Creator.

Plants, animals, and people regularly need to stop what they are doing, calm down, and reenergize, right? The darkness of the night was created to provide time to rest and balance daylight hours.

God gifted you with darkness as an opportunity to take advantage of living in the moment. You and all of God's creation need rest to prepare mentally and physically for the process of beginning a new day all over again (Psalm 62:1–2).

The absence of light is essential for people and animals. Abcnews.go.com states that humans and animals require darkness to produce melatonin, a hormone that tells the body it is time to rest. Melatonin can also help fight breast and prostate cancer in humans.

According to Sciencing.com, plants produce oxygen during the day but use it at night in a process called respiration. God made plants able to use darkness to grow, distribute chloroplasts, shape leaves, and continue daily cycles (Psalm 147:8). Plants grow in the hours before the sun comes up and use daytime hours to absorb light.

God designed the darkness of night to help predators and prey move or fly around more covertly. Nocturnal animals have a completely different life cycle than animals functioning during the daytime (Psalm 104:20).

These animals peruse when it is dark and sleep during the day. Owls, foxes, raccoons, skunks, and moths all sleep during the day and are active at night. Their keen sense of hearing, smell, and eyesight allows them to perform well in the dark.

Some humans seem to think they fall into this category as well. We always told our kids that nothing good happens after midnight!

Lightning bugs or fireflies are my favorite summer insects that emerge at night. In our younger days, my cousins and I would run around in the field, catching them. Carefully placing the soft beetles in a jar, we would watch them miraculously light up the glass.

After a few hours, we released the fireflies to fly away back into the night. Carefully, we followed them with our eyes as they fluttered away into the darkness, watching their lights to see which plants they would land on in the dark.

God's beautiful lights for us to see and experience at night are a blessing.

God designed your eyes to require the process of light so that you can see in more ways than one. Without the darkness of night, it would be impossible for you to believe in the benefits of light. The eyes represent where your attention is and what areas you concentrate on.

"The eye is a light for the body. If your eyes are good, your whole body will be full of light. But if your eyes are evil, your whole body will be full of darkness. And if the only light you have is really darkness, then you have the worst darkness" (Matthew 6:22–24).

Jesus is the focal point of God's Word and all creation so that your eyes can see His presence and feel rested (Colossians 1:15–17). God's Son, Jesus, is the constant light of the world and for your soul. When Jesus walked on the earth, He was divine and human. Jesus said, "I am the light of the world. The person who follows me will never live in darkness but will have the light that gives life" (John 8:12).

When Jesus said this, He was in the temple, where candles burned to represent God's pillar of fire. God's light led the people of Israel through the dark wilderness all those years; they were not lost. Jesus symbolizes the pillar of fire, which signifies God's protection, guidance, and presence, providing you and me with peace.

William Shakespeare, who often inspired his plays by the Bible, wrote, "The eyes are windows to the soul."

Jesus's light is a gift. When coming out of the darkness of night and into His light, we can see ourselves as we indeed are (Colossians 1:13–14). Some may not want their lives exposed to God's light because of what will be revealed (Job 34:22). Individuals must be willing to change their ways and believe.

If you are navigating dark, uncertain life situations, look toward the heavens. If you awake at night struggling with thoughts, locate the moon and stars through the window. Better yet, go outside.

Sit on the front step beneath the heavenly lights and talk with the Creator. God is the same sovereign God that led the Israelites through the darkness years ago. God didn't go anywhere.

Instead of telling others about your problems, talk to

Jesus like you would a friend. Jesus is the wisdom of God (1 Corinthians 1:30). He is a Wonderful Counselor who is always willing to listen (Isaiah 9:6). Jesus is the light of the world, a Prince of Peace, and wants to be your trusted friend who helps you to rest peacefully (Psalm 4:8).

I love sitting outside under the celestial stars and talking to God. The darkness makes me feel like we are alone together, just Him and me. Gazing up at the beauty of the bright lights above me, I talk to God about everything that is going on in my world.

We discuss what I am thinking and feeling as I continually ask him my many questions. When I need proof that God is listening, I ask to see a falling star. It is a very intimate experience between Him and me.

Even though God's face is not visible, His tangible presence repeatedly shines in the sky, connecting you to His love. He provides ways for you to see Him in the darkness as He shines His light ahead of you.

Anytime, anywhere in the world, day or night, the process of the heavenly lights shines for a purpose. Providing a way for you to see in the darkness, God's glorious love shines.

God provides you with proper rest because He loves you that much.

Trust His PCPR—Process, Connecting its Purpose of Repeating God's love and presence over and over.

Points to Ponder

What is one thing every living creature must have to survive?

CHAPTER 9

THE GIFT OF
WATER

God's spirit hovered over the water as the earth was formless and empty (Genesis 1:2). "Then God said, 'Let there be something to divide the water in two.' So, God made the air and placed some of the water above the air and some below it. God named the air 'sky'" (Genesis 1:6–8a). God told the waters beneath the sky to huddle together into one place, naming the waters "seas" (Genesis 1:10).

Resembling a mother bird caring for her young, God spoke creation into place and named it.

God formed the earth out of water and with water (Psalm 33:7). According to USGS.gov, 71 percent of the planet is water.

God made beaches to border the sea so the water could never go past (Psalm 104:9). The waves may pound the beach and roar but can't go beyond it (Jeremiah 5:22).

God made water with you in mind, reminding you that He is always nearby. Every time you drink water throughout the day, wipe off the kitchen counter, or wash your hands, realize that the water you are using is a gift that connects you with

God's presence.

Counting the many times you use water daily can be overwhelming. Can you imagine life without it?

One of the reasons God created and engineered the clear liquid is to make you clean and comfortable. You might walk over to flip on the shower as your feet hit the floor first thing in the morning.

Your mind distinguishes the rushing sound of the wonderful, warm water to transport you back to life. It is genuinely a fantastic present from God that I am incredibly thankful for. Right? Can you relate?

As a baby, my son hated water. Every night at bath time, he desperately clung to my arms, screaming as he tried to climb out of the tub. Moms, have you been there?

Sitting in the big tub of water by himself must have almost been torture to him. Bathing him was nearly impossible. I remember thinking, *How can this child go through life hating water this much? He is going to be dirty and smelly his whole life.*

As time passed, bathtub toys altered his perception, transforming his young attitude to appreciate water's purpose. Nowadays, he can't seem to get enough water. That boy of mine takes forever-long hot showers, and the lake is his favorite place in the summer.

How do you use God's gift of water? Your morning routine might look like mine. Get out of bed, drink water, fill the coffee pot with water, and turn it on. Flush the toilet, shower, cook your eggs, turn the dishwasher on, and brush your teeth. Can you see God's presence in your water usage throughout your day?

Water is a gift we cannot do life without and a precious, God-given resource we should not waste. When brushing your teeth, do you let the water faucet continually run? Try creating a new habit by turning the water off while brushing.

All of us have been assigned to care for this planet (Genesis 3:23).

God created water to be so much more than the substance in a clear plastic bottle or the liquid you carry all day. Water has a fantastic purpose as a natural resource that is clear, tasteless, odorless, and cannot be recreated.

The process of water is a remarkable and irreplaceable creation of God. The Almighty Creator designed everything on earth to depend upon water for life. Fueling many processes and cycles on earth, water repetitively keeps the planet you call home functioning.

Looking at the bigger picture of the earth, it's as if God made the process of water with a mind of its own. Amazingly, God designed the purpose of water to branch out and flow through veinous systems connecting throughout the earth. Even though you can't see it, water flows continuously above and below your feet. Everything in nature is connected.

USGS.gov explains that the process of water is directly connected to the sun. The sun is the driving force that repetitively moves the water you need around the earth. The process is called the water or hydrologic cycle and is solar powered.

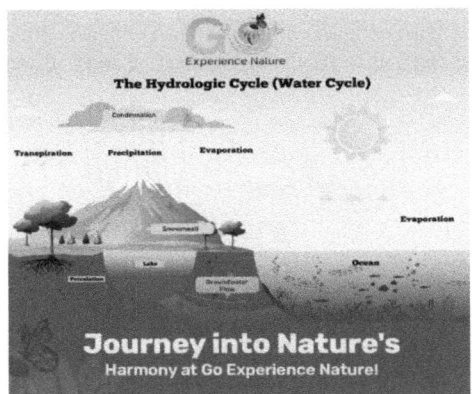

The cycle of water moving on the earth goes something like this. The sun initiates water to evaporate from lakes, rivers, and the ocean, causing it to rise into the atmosphere. The weather is affected as clouds and thunderstorms form.

Depending on the season, God provides moisture for your grass and flowers through rain, snow, or hail. God's intricately designed process repeats over and over again, continually providing moisture for the earth. Isn't that amazing?

God designed and connected rivers to keep underground aquifers, or bodies of water, complete and valuable. Water repetitively provides the earth with an irreplaceable environment for many plants and animals created by God to live in or near water.

Just like you and me, plants and animals continually drink water and are naturally attracted to it.

Every living thing is designed to need water as much as people need God. (Read that sentence again.)

The Almighty Creator crafted water's process to be invaluable to this planet and intimately connected to everything, just as He is. Only the God who creates these phenomena has the power to command and control their purpose (Job 38:28–30).

God created nature and repetitively uses water's energy in powerful and purposeful ways (Jeremiah 10:13). Water forms natural phenomena such as tropical cyclones, tsunamis, floods, landslides, blizzards, and thick fog. Only God completely understands and produces such events.

H_2O, the scientific name for water, is used for drinking, irrigation to grow food, and producing electricity for your house. It also plays a significant role in transporting merchandise worldwide. Water allows that item you purchase online to be delivered to your door.

Do you ever think about that? Water provides a very

functional source of transportation.

Recreating near "huddles of water" is one of my favorite summer activities. When I was growing up, the idea of going on a family vacation for a few days was not an option. Summertime is hectic for farmers, especially when cows are milked twice daily.

However, Grandma enjoyed planning special family event days. Each year, a couple of times during the summer, Grandma made sure we got away from the farm to have some fun. The time I looked forward to most was the day spent at a local water hole called Pete's Puddle.

Does your family love going to the lake? What are your favorite activities when you go?

Arriving after we finished chores, all the kids went straight to the paddle boats and canoes. Picking partners, we ventured into the designated lake area. Sometimes, we would change boat partners, chase each other around the island, make big waves for the next canoe, or pretend we had bumper boats. We were courteous and waved to the people fishing in the lake beside us.

By this time, the sun was high and hot in the sky. If lunch was not quite ready, we would unload the big black tractor tire inner tubes from the back of the pickup onto the sandy beach, then take a quick dip in the lake before eating.

The natural lake always had several twelve- to thirteen-foot tree logs floating in the water, just waiting for competition. The game's objective was to remain standing on the log for the longest time. You would run forward or backward, causing the log to spin so your competitor would lose their balance. The last person standing was the winner.

It sounds brutal, but it was great fun! It's so much better than looking at a screen.

You might get a bruise or two from slipping and falling, but comparing battle scars later in the week was even more fun as the stories only got better.

After lunch, it was time to try out the zip line. Climbing the wooden stairs barefoot was by far the worst part. Pure adrenaline pulsated through your veins while waiting to stand on the platform's edge and jump.

Hanging on for dear life as you sailed down the cable line while feeling the wind blow through your hair was amazing. Calculating the perfect moment to let go and drop into the water was the best feeling ever, a feeling of true accomplishment on a hot afternoon.

The entire family would then break out their swimsuits to get in the water. This was the only day that Dad and Grandpa's ghost-white legs ever saw daylight, and they walked outside with bare feet.

Their everyday attire was boots and jeans, which made it hilarious to watch them try to walk on the sand with their tender, exposed feet.

Tired and sunburned by late afternoon, we ended the day by enjoying watermelon. Placed in the pool of spring water first thing upon arrival, the melons were good and cold by afternoon.

Then we packed up and headed home to milk cows and do evening chores, ending a perfectly simple day of family: fresh air, sunshine, and water. Sometimes, it's the simple things that make life fun—hanging out with family and having a great time.

Water is free and illuminates God's presence, helping you to believe. You and I totally take water and God's presence for granted daily. H_2O is the most consumed natural resource that God created on the earth.

Usgs.gov states that the average US water use is sixty gallons per day. Your family uses 138 gallons in your household. You are very fortunate and blessed to have clean water to drink and grow food.

Many of us are totally spoiled and don't realize it. Ourworldindata.org explains that 29 percent of the world's population cannot access safe drinking water. When you have always had water to use, it is so easy to take it for granted.

Water used for agricultural purposes or farming comes from water in rivers and streams, groundwater from wells, and rainwater. Poor water quality can affect the quality of crops we grow for food and make the people who eat them sick. There is great concern worldwide over the rapidly depleted reserves of freshwater available all over the earth.

The Centers for Disease Control and Prevention advises that the best way to increase agricultural water use is to manage strategies to improve water efficiency without decreasing yields.

The miraculous, God-given liquid He named water gives life. It has life. God makes the process of moisture moving across the earth connect by picking up the natural benefits and properties of minerals and microbes as it flows.

There is a difference between living water and dead water. Living water is unprocessed water derived directly from nature and containing all its life-giving properties.

Unfortunately, the treated, distilled, and processed tap water we drink has had its life-giving properties removed and is essentially dead.

God made water's purpose to be an invaluable and life-sustaining force. Every living being is connected through their dependence on water's purpose, which is crucial for staying alive.

The average human body is 60 percent water. "Water allows

everything inside the body's cells to have the right shape at the molecular level," states sitn.hms.harvard.edu.

Your body is made with the ability to survive a month without food but would not survive three days without water.

God created water to be the universal solvent in its biological role. Water's repetitive process dissolves more substances than any other.

Water is a powerful influence and is persistent in its purpose. God gives every single drop of water the power to melt away rock. The drops can connect, creating a repetitive process of destructive force. Over time, the water process slowly carries away dirt and rock in a process called erosion.

God designed nature's purpose and process to connect and change repetitively. Nothing in nature is the status quo. Everything in nature changes, and your life follows the same path.

Nationalgeographic.org explains the purpose and power of water as it moves from reservoir to reservoir. Streams of water connecting and combining with gravity can create a mighty canyon. The incredible Grand Canyon in Arizona was created by the process and slow power of the water in the Colorado River carrying away rock and earth. This robust process happens over a long time, sometimes millions of years.

God gave water power and an influence of its own. Water connects into rivers, streams, lakes, and ponds, flowing repetitively downhill to the ocean.

A river is persistent with its purpose, always flowing forward, connecting in the same direction, and never turning around to flow in reverse.

You can learn many life lessons from water. Go with the flow, don't look back, be calm and let things settle.

Water's power seems to grasp our minds. People crave

the magnanimous sounds of crashing waves over rocks with seagulls screeching as they fly overhead. Infatuated with the stunning shades of blue, we long to enjoy the peaceful beauty of water as it soothes our soul and well-being.

People are willing to pay the price of living near the water for the comforting effects of captivating blue waters. Homelight. com explains that oceanfront properties sell nearly 45 percent more than homes not on the water.

I was an adult before I experienced the ocean. Flowing seas of native grass and colorful wildflowers have always surrounded my Kansas farm home. Growing up, I longed to witness the wet, salty waves of ocean water.

Somewhere in my late twenties, between business meetings near the coast, I enjoyed my first visit to the beach. It was a lifelong dream for a farm girl born and raised in the Midwest.

I smelled the ocean air, watched seagulls, and tasted salt on my lips. With each cell of my body, I felt the fullness of being alive in the moment. I was mesmerized and felt connected by watching the fluid movement of such a large body of water.

Driven by wind, the waves work together to create chaos, with water moving in every direction. Listening to the loud waves crashing on the sand and producing their rhythm made me feel small in comparison. I was humbled and completely in awe of God's immense power before me.

Can you relate? Do you remember your first visit to see the ocean?

Ninety-seven percent of the water on earth is salt water, explains Sciencing.com. Imagine the complexity of the repetitive process God designed to keep all the salt water on earth just the right saltiness. This process totally maintains all animal life connected in the world of the sea.

God created the ocean to provide a unique and different

environment for sea life compared to animals on land. Www. trafalgar.com states that 94 percent of animal species living on earth live in the ocean.

Ocean animals come in every shape and size, from microscopic to massive. Some are even kind of funny looking. Fish and many other marine animals make their homes in all parts of the sea, including the seafloor. Yet they all live peacefully together (Psalm 69:34), a great lesson we can learn from nature.

God created each drop of water to be separate, just like you and me. Yet, when many drops are "huddled together," they form a body of water that can hold a massive ship. God made the ocean to illustrate how people can work together to accomplish amazing things.

"There is power in unity, and there is power in numbers" (Dr. Martin Luther King Jr.).

I am so thankful that God meticulously and repetitively continues to create and maintain the process of the ocean's peaceful purpose on earth (Habakkuk 2:14). God is always working in the background of nature as it functions. It's no wonder God never sleeps (Psalm 92:2).

In Job chapter 38, we hear God asking Job questions about the purpose and process of how nature was created. "Who shut the doors to keep the sea in when it broke through and was born? When I said to the sea, 'You may come this far, but no farther; this is where your proud waves must stop'" (vs. 8, 11).

God asked questions to remind Job that He uses his mighty power according to His impeccable moral perfection. God is, by nature, perfect (Matthew 5:48). All of creation's purposes and processes are connected and repetitively depend upon God for their existence. God has power over the universe because He created it (Jeremiah 10:12).

All of creation listens to its creator. The Almighty Creator commands the forces of nature by releasing or restraining them with His mighty power at will. Matthew 14 tells how Jesus controlled the laws of nature by feeding five thousand people with only five loaves of bread and two fish.

Later that night, Jesus walked on water to help His struggling disciples caught in a boat out in a storm (Psalm 77:19). The disciples thought they were seeing a ghost until Jesus spoke to them. The presence of Jesus calmed their fears.

Matthew 8 describes another time when Jesus and the disciples were in a boat on the lake when a nasty storm emerged. Jesus was exhausted and sleeping hard, so the frightened disciples woke Him up to help them (Matthew 8:25).

Have you ever been in a deep sleep when someone frantically wakes you up? You might be disorientated and not even know where you are. Happiness is probably not the first emotion you wake up with, right? Especially when you realize the useless reason they woke you.

Jesus was a human on the earth and might have been a bit crabby when the disciples suddenly woke Him. Jesus asked His students in the boat, "Dude, why are you so afraid? Where is your faith?" Then He stood up in the rocking boat and told the wind and waves to cut it out and chill (Matthew 8:26).

Like you tell your kids when they get out of hand in the car's back seat, Jesus didn't even need to repeat Himself. The tone of His voice said it all. The wind and waves stopped their chaos the first time He told them.

Jesus has that kind of power because He brought the wind and water into this world, and only He can take them out. He created them (Psalm 89:9).

The wind and waves respond because they recognize Jesus as the Almighty Creator. Jesus is the only one with the authority to command water and all of nature. You can know and believe that the presence of Jesus is the solution to your fear.

When bad things happen, and life doesn't make sense, you and I only see what directly affects us. Our view is a very minute part of the whole purpose and process.

Whatever God does is fair because He repetitively connects the entire big picture of His plan to show His love. Don't let your fears get ahold of you and win. Trust God; He will do what is right for you (2 Samuel 22:31).

You will repetitively experience moments that make you feel scared, but you don't need to live continually feeling that way. Water represents life, a symbol for salvation and actual knowledge of God, Jesus, and the Holy Spirit (Revelation 22:1).

Water can purify. The Holy Spirit's presence will cleanse and sanctify your heart because you are a child of God (John 1:12). As a believer, you can be baptized in water, representing the purification of the soul and declaring your faith (Luke 3:3).

You need physical and spiritual "living water" that only Jesus can give. You will have rivers of living water constantly flowing forward from within you (John 7:37–39).

Jesus answered, "Everyone who drinks this water will be thirsty again, but whoever drinks the water I give will never be thirsty. The water I give will become a spring of water gushing up inside that person, giving eternal life" (John 4:13–14).

Think of the Creator with every drink of water you take and believe. Let the water bottle you carry daily remind you that Jesus is always with you. If you ask Him, Jesus will continually live in your heart and provide living water that offers eternal life (Revelation 3:20).

Expect His presence to be with you always, and you will overcome your fears. Let Jesus's well-watered promise of peace saturate your soul with purpose and satisfy your deepest needs (Numbers 6:26).

Point to Ponder

What determines where you build your house, some of your favorite outdoor activities, and the type of crops grown for food?

CHAPTER 10

EARTH'S HOLY
FOUNDATION

*I*n God's design for earth, land and water are the primary building blocks of the planet you live on.

Everything you do is structured in, on, or around these elements. NASA tells us that land makes up 29 percent of the earth.

The book of Genesis defines precise details of how God used a process to create.

God commanded the water under the sky to "gather together" and connect for the specific purpose of dry land appearing (Genesis 1:9). Obeying God's command, creation transpired, and it materialized.

God named the created dry land "Earth."

Soil is alive and provides life. Daily, you walk on God's created earth with each step.

According to Phys.Org, "Soil is the most species-rich ecosystem in the world. Two-thirds of all species live in the soil."

Farmers and folks involved in agribusiness make their livelihood from living off the land. All wealth comes from land.

Being a farmer's daughter, I have always heard that buying land is the best investment you will ever make.

Land is a natural asset whose value has increased over time. A tangible asset, land does not require remodeling, such as a house, but correct management and upkeep. Its purpose is flexible and can be used in many ways.

When I was a young girl living on my family's farm, I was jealous of the kids in town. I longed to cruise around, sailing along paved streets and riding my royal blue bicycle with a sparkly white banana seat on the pavement. Riding my bike on the rough gravel roads I lived on was almost impossible.

I often wondered what it would be like to live in town, especially when hauling irrigation pipe at five o'clock on early summer mornings. I decided one thing was for sure. I was not going to marry a farmer.

Nature provides resources with a purpose to be used the way God intended. Depending on the location and natural resources available, you need land for hiking, swimming in a lake, or fishing in a stream.

Land use is connected to and goes hand in hand with people's desires and demands. God made soil's purpose so amazing that it can be changed to express people's wishes and show the influence of environmental factors.

People can manipulate the land to build skyscrapers and manufacturing facilities, build homes, and grow food. However, land is an irreplaceable resource with limited amounts available.

God is not making anymore.

Land use can be used in several different ways, as explained by study.com.

Five Common Ways to Use Land

Residential. Providing a place for you to live.

Agricultural. Growing food for you and animals to eat. Wheat, corn, livestock, fruits, and vegetables are all grown using the land.

Recreational. A fantastic way to get outside and soak up some vitamin D while enjoying swimming, fishing, or hiking in a stress-free environment.

Transportation. Movement of people, animals, or goods from one location to another. It can be accomplished by human—or animal-powered transport, rail, or road transport.

Commercial. Businesses use the land to manufacture products. Then they sell goods and services that generate income to provide a livelihood for people.

Land is more connected to your lifestyle than you may realize. God designed the amazing earth you live on, with many types of land formations providing a variety of choices for places to call home.

You decide where you want to live based on your favorite features of the terrain, climate, and temperature.

The landscape surrounding you influences your outdoor activities and the type of house you build.

Soil type is directly connected to and determines the crops and food grown for food.

Have you ever thought about how land determines where you live? Your life revolves around natural resources. Everything in nature works together.

God's designed process of changing the landscape can take up to a few hours or expand to millions of years.

The terrain is sculpted and naturally formed repetitively on the earth by connections with the wind, water, ice, and the earth's interior movement.

Landforms determine the climate, lifestyles, resources, and

plants for people and the animals living on or in them.

You can choose your preference and live on any land formation that makes you feel comfortable. Standing barefoot with my toes buried on a white, sandy beach while listening to the ocean roar provides me with such peace.

For someone else, standing on the wide-open plains looking out as far as their eyes can see may calm their mind. My friend loves hiking in the mountains and sleeping in a tent.

The cool, fresh air can help you feel calm and tranquil, as you are collectively part of something much bigger than yourself. God's earth is so impressive.

Schooltutoring.com explains the different types of land formations.

Nine Common Physical Features on the Earth

Mountains. Landforms higher than the surrounding areas. Mountains and hills are formed by tectonic plate movement under the earth.

Plateaus. Flat highlands that are separated from the surroundings by steep slopes.

Valleys. Low areas of land lying between hills and mountains. They have been formed by water from rivers and glaciers for millions of years.

Deserts. Due to inadequate rainfall, the land is hot and dry with little or no vegetation.

Dunes. Small sandhills formed by the flow of water underground.

Islands. Land surrounded by water caused by volcanic activity or a hotspot from heat deep in the earth. The string of Hawaiian Islands formed from a hot spot in the Pacific plate.

Plains. Flat areas on the surface of the earth. Dirt, rock, and sediment are deposited by wind, water, and ice erosion.

Rivers. Freshwater streams naturally flow from mountains toward other rivers, lakes, and oceans.

Glaciers. Large bodies of ice formed by layers of snow located in high mountains and polar regions. Gravity and pressure cause them to move.

In all types of terrain, God repetitively provides rocks and stones made from minerals.

Let's say you are anxious or nervous about something like speaking in front of a group. Find a little rock you can hold as a solid reminder of God's presence.

If you feel uneasy, slip your hand into your pocket and hold onto the keepsake. God will never leave you. God's presence is always near because God is your rock (Psalm 18:2).

God's process of land and water needs each other and repetitively connects to be healthy so that the water cycle works efficiently.

The water process connected with the purpose of land provides the basis for all living things to live, grow, and exist. God designed healthy soil to act as a holding tank and absorb and store water for the plants in your garden.

You are gifted with the ability to grow plants, raise animals, and produce food because of God's bio-grace. Through nature, God provides the life-giving power so that humans and animals can eat and help maintain the earth.

Keith Berns with Green Cover conceived the term bio-grace. The term describes the grace God provides through the biology of nature, gifted in healthy soil. You and I have done nothing to earn or deserve it. God's bio-grace is provided freely, is unlimited, and will never run out.

Do you like to grow a garden or an orchard? You can plant seeds in the ground and ensure they have water, sunshine, and healthy soil, but God gives life to the seeds.

God enables and connects you to do more than you could on your own. You and I can't give life to pigs, leaves, earthworms, or sunflowers, but God does. God provides this unmerited favor of bio-grace to you for a purpose.

God has gifted all creation with natural resources, such as solar energy, carbon, nitrogen, minerals and nutrients, soil biology, and water. We have been gifted much to work with, and we should cultivate the earth correctly to maintain healthy soil.

Soil health repetitively influences water, plants, minerals, animals, and you.

Many things we cannot see work hard using their purpose to take care of the earth. Earthworms create healthy soil by repetitively recycling organic materials. They have an essential purpose—eating fungi and connecting leftover crop residue to improve soil and water filtration.

Farmer George provides a fun example of how he used the connected process of bio-grace in nature to fix an area on his farm that was a mess. His story is a true testimonial confirming that everything God created and designed in nature relates to and connects to healthy soil.

Farmer George needed to fix an overgrown area on his farm encumbered with tall, viny, ground-covering weeds tangled together. Being a smart man, the farmer built a pen around the entire weedy mess for his pigs. The pigs loved their new space, and their daily activities cleaned up the whole area.

Next, the farmer mixed grass seeds in the pig's feed. The pigs fertilized the area and planted seeds as they pooped, walked around, and rolled in the pen.

Nature repetitively provides a connected chain of events involving plants, animals, soil, sunshine, and water, helping Farmer George to think smarter instead of working harder. He was rewarded for using a natural process that God had already designed.

Healthy soil and God's bio-grace allow insects and earthworms to perform their God-given purpose. NRCS. USDA.gov states that one acre of healthy soil contains one million earthworms constantly pulling residue into their burrows to improve soil health.

Occasionally, I deliver seeds grown on our farm to other farms and businesses in Kansas. I am convinced that God definitely has a sense of humor. Even after stating many times that I would not marry a farmer, I am a farmer's wife.

Imagine for a moment if God had not provided the process of directions for traveling and getting around on His earth.

A very concise part of God's plan is His universal directions. Physics-Network.org explains that cardinal directions, north, south, east, and west, are essential directions people use worldwide.

The Earth rotates from west to east, thus causing the sun to rise in the east and set in the west. Cardinal directions use the rising and setting of the sun as reference points.

Earth and the land you know would be chaotic and challenging to navigate without God's pivotal directions (Genesis 13:14). The internet is man-made and will never be totally dependable. Yet many rely heavily on cell phones to tell us where to go.

There are many locations in Kansas where my cell phone can't get a signal, making GPS and maps worthless. I travel with a paper map and print directions ahead of time as a backup, or I will be lost.

What if the internet crashed and your cell phone no longer functioned? Do you recognize directions?

Can you think logically enough to return to the basics and use nature for directions and time? Do you have a printed copy of your contacts?

The sun's location in the sky can show you the approximate time of day. At noon, the sun is high in the sky. The sun can help you navigate directions if you know your surroundings.

Remember that the sun rises in the east and sets in the west. Knowing the basics of nature can help you navigate and get to where you are going.

Practice locating which direction is north, south, east, and west. Someday, you might be glad you did.

The things God gives and provides for you enlighten aspects of His personality and what He must be like. Psalm 103:12 explains how God uses His power to remove your sin as far as the east is from the west. God loves you that much.

The east and west will never meet, supporting infinite space. This means God loves you so much that He removes your sins as far away as you can possibly imagine. He will never bring up your past failures or heartache; it is up to you to let them go and forget.

PCPR explains that God's power repetitively connects the process of everything created with a purpose on His earth. There are many days you and I still like to think we are in charge; however, life is never about only you or me.

God repetitively controls the purpose and process of the earth and land in its entirety. You do not need to worry or fear. Trust God. Believe in Him.

God's control is physically apparent in the winds of a tornado, an earthquake, wildfires, strikes of lightning, or a volcanic eruption. Scientists might have names and explanations for how these natural phenomena occur, but they still can't completely predict or stop them from happening.

The Almighty Creator completely controls nature, and we do not. Don't worry; God has a plan.

God reminded Job that He commands all the forces of nature and can unleash or restrain them at His will.

"Have you ever gone into the storehouse of the snow or seen the storehouses of hail, for which I save for the times of trouble, for days of war and battle? Where is the place from which light comes? Where is the place from which the east winds blow over the earth? Who sends rain to satisfy the empty land, so the grass begins to grow?" (Job 38:22–24, 27).

God's point was that if Job could not explain the everyday events in nature, how could he possibly explain or question the process or purpose of God? Job could not perhaps understand God's endless resources. You and I can't either.

Whatever God does is fair, even if you don't understand. Friend, I don't know about you, but there are many times when my heart hurts, and I do the same thing as Job. I question God and His authority.

It's okay to tell God your frustrations. He can take it because He already knows what you are thinking anyway. God sees your struggles and listens to your fears. He wants you to lean on Him.

God already knows your need to be rescued. He knows the home of the east wind and will walk out to you during your storm (Matthew 15:25–27).

The spirit of the Lord will help you in your weakness (Romans 8:26–28). Seeing His presence in nature will help to connect you and close the distance between you and Him.

You and I live in the repetitive process of our own little world. We assume everyone else has the same connection to our normal.

The older I get, the more I realize it is not true. Everyone is connected to their own type of normal for a purpose. Most of the time, we seem oblivious, not knowing what we don't know, but thankfully, God knows.

When I worked for the state fair, our staff provided classes for the local third- and fourth-grade schoolchildren during National Agriculture Week.

I taught a class about animals. A donkey stood behind me, tied to the livestock trailer. A little boy ran up to me as the kids rotated to the next group. With great excitement, he pointed toward the animal behind me. His face was beaming as he exclaimed how cool the camel was.

I smiled and told him it was a donkey. After two more kids did the same thing, I turned around to ensure someone hadn't switched the animal behind me.

I was surprised by the children's comments. These kids were from a small town in Kansas. Raised a farm kid, I had always just assumed all kids in Kansas could identify animals.

During the presentation, I asked the kids where milk comes from. A few hands went up with an answer. I pointed to a child, and her answer was from the store. Several children had no idea. I explained that a cow made milk, and many were shocked.

After class, a couple of teachers admitted they had learned something. They didn't know where the milk came from. They had never thought about it.

This truly shocked me. I grew up milking cows daily at my grandparents' dairy, less than ten miles from where I taught this class. I struggled with the reality of people living in a town only a few miles from where I grew up, not knowing where their food came from.

I taught this class for several years. Each year, I experienced the same story.

What if transportation systems broke down and the grocery store became empty? Would you be able to grow food to feed your family?

Trying to decide what to purchase for the evening meal might be your biggest issue when you stop by the grocery store after work, right? If you are in a hurry and time is short, plenty of drive-throughs exist.

Maybe food has always been readily available, and you have never considered how food gets to the store. You have never thought about how food grows because you have never needed to.

FarmBureau.org states that the average American is at least three generations removed from the farm. That means your family hasn't raised a steer or grown a watermelon in almost one hundred years.

The purpose of the land God provides is the essential foundation for the process of growing food while connecting and sustaining the world.

Six hundred and ninety million people, roughly 8.9 percent of the population in the world, go to bed hungry every night, shares Worldvision.org. Yet farmers grow enough food to feed one and a half times the world's population.

Medium.com shares that 30 to 40 percent of food worldwide is wasted. Unfortunately, lower-developed countries lack the knowledge and equipment to keep food fresh and refrigerated.

In more developed countries, food portions increase with super-sized meals, intensifying food waste.

Since the very beginning of time, God has given humans the responsibility of taking care of the land, growing and providing food for their own families and themselves. The Farm Bureau states that farm and ranch families comprise less than 2 percent of the US population.

Farm and ranch families work from sunup to sundown daily, no matter the weather, to provide and produce food for 100 percent of the population. These exceptionally hardworking people will do their best, but ultimately, they are not entirely responsible for feeding everyone.

Learning to protect and take care of our precious, God-given soil is imperative.

Predictions show that land could return to the same state as it was in the Dust Bowl era in the early 1930s. If the same fertilizer, herbicide, and tillage practices continue, the problem could recur in as little as fifteen years.

How you and I take care of the land determines if and how the land will take care of us.

Near Casey, Iowa, along I-80, there is a fascinating exhibit showing the amount of topsoil in their state.

Soilsolution.net explains that in 1850, the amount of topsoil was fourteen inches. Over the years, it continued to decrease, decreasing to 5.5 inches from 1950 to 2000.

It is a sobering display of where we are heading. This only proves that serious change needs to be made.

Land is a precious God-given resource we cannot afford to take for granted any longer. We must teach our children and grandchildren a way of life and process that values and improves nature and all creation.

Legacy is about taking care of what we have. Future generations of plants, animals, and people depend upon and are connected to soil health.

Soil needs to be alive and working at its full potential to continue the process of life.

"As sure as we are given the gift to share moments with our friends and family in God's natural world, we are as indebted to pass along a spirit of stewardship to those who follow" (Johnny Morris).

God designed healthy soil to be alive. Without biology, it is just geology. Photosynthesis is a natural process that generates life, creating the difference between dirt and soil.

How can you teach your children or grandchildren how to care for the land? Growing a garden or fruit trees is an excellent project for kids to help with.

Extension.oregonstate.edu explains that dirt has two components, physical and chemical.

Plant biology transforms dirt into soil using sunlight, moisture, and CO_2. Healthy soil is full of many life-containing organisms.

One teaspoon of healthy soil contains a billion bacteria, fungal filaments, thousands of protozoa, and nematodes. Everything in nature works together.

You will repetitively experience the purpose and process of God's loving faithfulness in many ways when you are connected to nature.

It is easy to overlook or take the gifts you have come to expect for granted. One is the blessing of healthy soil and fertile land as the earth's foundation.

God sent Eve's relatives out to work the land you were made from. How are you doing your part?

Today's farming process is beginning to look much different from in the past. Conservation and agriculture are working together.

We now understand the adverse effects of repetitively using heavy equipment to process and completely clear debris from a field each year.

Farmers are learning a new way of thinking. Regenerative farming uses God's purpose and process of nature at its best. God has had a plan since creation began.

Regenerative farming uses stubble and material from previous crops remaining in the field, connecting them to improve soil health and slow erosion. Removing plants and stalks from previous crops leaves the soil bare, reducing soil health.

My farmer husband and many other farmers and ranchers worldwide have a true passion for regenerating God-given land that they were unknowingly taught to mismanage. Over time, they are working to conserve the land and water that all life depends upon.

Farmers are making a difference by rebuilding soil health, teaching young farmers the purpose of what they are learning, and continually improving soil for many generations to come.

"Conquest of the Land Through 7,000 Years" is a study by Dr. Walter Clay Lowdermilk from 1938 to 1939. His mission was to examine older civilizations worldwide, looking for answers to help solve current land-use problems in the United States. He noted that land provides water and nourishment for food grown from the earth.

Dr. Lowdermilk discovered that the land richly rewards the perceptive and diligent but penalizes the oblivious and lazy. He noted that neglect of the land could topple empires and wipe out entire civilizations, such as Kish and Babylon.

In the Old Testament Bible days, many areas were lush green gardens, but because of man, they are now desert lands. If you and I learn to take care of the land using good stewardship of the earth's resources, it will allow many societies to succeed for centuries.

The repetitive purpose and process of terracing, crop rotation, and other soil conservation measures are imperative for improving soil health and continuing a partnership that establishes the foundation for even today's complex social structure. Rest easy knowing God still allows land and farmers to connect.

While pondering many years of land use issues, Dr. Lowdermilk wrote the Eleventh Commandment. He thought that if Moses had anticipated what would happen to the Promised Land in three thousand years, he would have established the direction for man's relation to the earth. Dr. Lowdermilk's "Eleventh Commandment" is as follows:

> Thou shalt inherit the Holy Earth as a faithful steward, conserving its resources and productivity from generation to generation. Thou shalt safeguard thy fields from soil erosion, thy living waters from drying up, thy forests from desolation, and protect thy hills from overgrazing by the herds, that thy descendants may have abundance forever. If any shall fail in this stewardship of the land, thy fruitful fields shall become sterile stony ground and wasting gullies, and thy descendants shall decrease and live in poverty or perish from off the face of the earth.

All land, along with the gift of bio-grace, belongs to God and is a physical inheritance from Him. Land has always been important to God's covenant with His people. It is not just a commodity (Psalm 37:29).

In the Old Testament, God's relationship with His people was directly linked to the land He graciously gave them to live on. The faithful were obedient and occupied the land, providing for their families.

To dwell in the Lord's land was to dwell with the Lord. Even today, God's presence still dwells with us in the land and nature.

The land conveys and connects a critical purpose and position in the Bible. Beginning with Genesis, Adam and Eve lived in a garden connected to God's presence.

Beginning in Revelation, believers will be repetitively connected to the purpose and process of living with God in the new heaven and the new earth. Everything in between shows the developmental process of faith and belief in God's people on the earth He created.

God gifted the Israelites with land they did not have to work for and cities they did not have to build. He provided vineyards and olive trees they did not plant (Joshua 23:16). Even today, you and I are gifted just like the Israelites.

Many generations are entirely removed from farming. Some folks are so far away from farming and nature that, sadly, they completely miss out on the benefits nature offers them. Has God gifted you the ability to eat food you did not grow?

You and I are descendants of Adam and Eve. We are instilled with responsibility and a connected purpose of caring for the holy Earth named and gifted to us by our heavenly Father (Genesis 3:23). Everything in nature was created and named by God to help you believe in Him. He gave you and me the garden to take care of.

God created and connected you to land to enjoy His excellent natural resources, providing a magnificent planet to live on. We are all in this together. Life is never about only you.

Take care of the natural resources and gifts you are blessed with. Teach the next generation to leave the land better than they have received.

Point to Ponder

Are plants important to the earth?

CHAPTER 11

PETALS, LEAVES, AND EVERYTHING GREEN

I am so thankful that God created plants with a meticulous design on the third day.

In His plan, the earth is gifted with oceans of grass and seas of trees. Can you imagine living on the earth without flowers, trees, shrubbery, and vegetation?

When God created, He had a strategy and named all the parts as He explained them. God said, "Let the earth produce plants, some to make grain for seeds and others to make fruits with seeds in them. Every seed will produce more of its own kind of plant" (Genesis 1:11).

God's "seed plan" to provide food has occurred accurately and precisely from generation to generation since the very first plant was grown. The plan has not changed. Even today, plants continually highlight God's presence. God's blueprint for seeds can solidify belief.

God designed plants to be beautiful, colorful, and valuable (Genesis 1:30). God's colorful plants are a part of creation that repetitively connects their purpose to many different aspects of nature's big picture. It is challenging to grasp the power plants have on our planet.

Foliage, or plants with leaves, are incredible creations that benefit your life. While adding beauty to the earth, plants provide oxygen, shade, clothing, shelter, medicine, and many other things. Plants provide food for insects, animals, and you. Without plants, our planet would not function (Isaiah 61:11).

Some plants are designed to live underwater in ponds, rivers, and lakes. God's design ensures that aquatic plants help balance the ecosystem.

Plankton grows in the ocean and is a food source for many sea animals. Many other plants also grow in the ocean through photosynthesis. Oceanservice.noaa.gov estimates that roughly half of the oxygen production on earth comes from the sea.

Scienceinpublic.com states that your life on earth is only possible because of the repetitive connection to plants.

- Plant roots help to protect soil from floods and drought.
- Animals depend on plants for food.
- People would not survive without animals or plants.

Although we like to think we are, people are not in charge. The Master of the Universe oversees everything.

Thank God that humans don't run this planet. Can you imagine what would happen to nature if people were in charge?

Only God provides healthy soil for plants to grow, fashions fruit with seeds, and blesses seeds with potential life inside.

God created plants to be living things a lot like you and me (Psalm 92:12–14). If you think about it, the life processes of plants and humans both involve the following:

- Movement.
- Eating healthy food.

- Drinking water.
- Breathing.
- Capturing sunlight.
- Communication.
- Growth.
- Making more of our kind.
- The life cycle of a plant begins with a tiny seed that contains DNA, just like people and animals.

When God created, He purposely used a specific order and process. He made soil, plants, animals, and then people. Many of the same processes are shared and used by all.

One example is that people have the same microbes or bacteria in their gut and internal organs as healthy soil. Plants and animals have the same microbes as well.

The Bible explains how this happened:

- Genesis 2:9 says, "The Lord God caused every beautiful tree and every tree that was good for food to grow out of the ground."
- Genesis 2:19 says, "From the ground, God formed every wild animal and every bird in the sky."
- Genesis 2:7 says, "Then the Lord God took dust from the ground and formed a man from it."

We are all connected; you are part of nature and connected to where you live.

Do you notice trees? I mean, get up close, study, and really look at them? Trees are magnificent creations that can totally be taken for granted. It is so easy to overlook the beauty of nature. You can continually walk past the same things daily without seeing them, which then becomes a habit.

Look at the leaves on trees and notice the tiny details; be

intentional. Observe the rugged and rough bark that protects the tree. Focus on how the minute veins running through the leaf continually supply the nutrients it needs to remain alive. Think of how that leaf is a part of and connects to the enormous tree's bark, flowers, and entire underground root system.

The US Forest Service explains that the tree's outer bark is continually renewed from within. The bark helps keep moisture from the rain out yet prevents the tree from losing moisture when the air is dry. It also serves as insulation against cold and heat and fights off insects. The bark is coarse and bumpy, yet the leaf on a tree is delicate and beautiful.

God made trees for many reasons (Isaiah 61:3b). Think of all the critters, birds, squirrels, bugs, and cicadas that live in and around trees.

The tree provides shade for you, shelter for animals, and wood for houses. It creates oxygen and grows beautiful leaves. Every reason that the tree is there is a God-provided purpose. Every day, the tree is alive; it serves its purpose for creation, just like you and me (Proverbs 3:18).

God will provide what you need to face whatever situation life brings. Just as bark on a tree is continually renewed from within, God will do the same thing for you.

God has placed you exactly where you are for a purpose and will provide you with what you need (Psalm 1:3). Friend, you can let go of your fears.

God created many types of foliage because He loves you and wants you to believe in Him. Green and blue are stunningly beautiful together. Maybe that is why God designed plants with so many shades of green, to highlight the lovely hue of the blue sky and brilliant waters.

"It gives me great delight to think of my soul as a garden in which the Lord came to walk about," said Mother Teresa.

Healthy plants, such as trees, breathe in what you breathe out. Plants breathe carbon dioxide and breathe out oxygen. You breathe in what the trees breathe out, a connected design of God. He totally created the repetitive process.

Trees in the forest evolve to live cooperatively, repetitively helping each other out. In the article "Do Trees Talk to Each Other?" *Science-Smithsonian* magazine explains that trees share water and nutrients through networks that can be used to communicate.

Trees create community and send distress signals to alert each other of drought, disease, and insect attacks through what scientists call mycorrhizal networks. They also communicate distress signals through the air by sending pheromones and other scent signals to warn nearby trees of the giraffe that is eating its leaves. Scientific studies confirm that other trees change and alter their behavior after receiving the messages.

Trees are repetitively consistent in their purpose of producing the kind of fruit God created them to grow. As believers, do we do the same thing?

Do our words and actions radiate the truths of scripture that God wants us to share with others? Can we be identified as believers by how we live our lives?

Jesus explained, "Grapes don't come from thornbushes, and figs don't come from thorny weeds. In the same way, every good tree produces good fruit, but a bad tree produces bad fruit" (Matthew 7:18).

A question we should all ponder is, can people identify my roots of faith by the flowers and leaves of my actions?

Have you ever eaten a peach picked right off the tree? Does it taste any different from the fruit from a grocery store shelf?

A ripe peach picked fresh from the tree is the best-tasting peach ever. Like fruit chosen from a branch in the Word of

God, the Bible is the best place to get advice, connect with Him, and process information to live life.

Simply sharing the words of God that you read from the Bible with others will help God's kingdom to grow.

After eating a piece of fruit, keep the seed. Wash and dry the seeds. Store them in a bag and leave them in your car. Try tossing the seed out the window in an area without trees when driving.

Nature will take care of the process itself. This practice has existed for centuries in Asian countries. You are helping fruit trees to grow everywhere for those who need something to eat (2 Corinthians 9:6).

God engineered plants with a process to reproduce themselves. In God's plan, the plant will grow and mature to produce flowers and seeds for food.

Amazingly, every tiny seed holds the miracle of giving life to a baby plant with leaves, a stem, and roots. You can dig a hole, cover it with healthy soil, and wait. Sunshine and water play their part as you watch for it to sprout, but God gives it life.

Farmers never really know precisely when a crop will be ready to harvest until it's ready. Typically, there is a small window of time to work in before the weather changes the plan.

Harvest is a beautiful time for gathering crops, representing a farmer's hard work for the year (John 4:37). However, it can also be very stressful on a farm.

I remember a big summer thunderstorm heading our way when I was in high school. It was a hot Saturday afternoon during the wheat harvest. Dad was determined to finish a couple of fields before the rain began.

Mom and I arrived at the field to help. Two loaded trucks were ready and waiting, and combines were working to fill the third. We quickly crawled into the first truck. I was driving and would drop Mom off near the second loaded truck.

Two mice came running from under the seat and around our feet when we pulled out of the field onto the dirt road. I slammed on the brake, took the truck out of gear, and bailed out the door. Mom jumped out her side as well.

The truck was still slowly rolling forward as Mom and I did a silly mouse dance on the road.

Little did we know that Dad had witnessed the entire scene from the combine he was operating. Stopping and jumping out, he ran across the field, thinking the truck must be on fire. While dancing, we realized Dad was standing behind us, panting, trying to shout something about a fire extinguisher.

Mom was already pulling on my arm when I began to explain we had jumped out because of the mice running around our feet. She kept saying, "Get in the truck and drive, Deb."

We can look back on that time now and laugh, but at that moment, Dad was not very happy with us. He could have yelled and thrown a big tantrum. Instead, he turned around and stomped back to the combine, shaking his head and talking to himself the whole way back.

The way you respond to life when it happens highlights your faith not only in yourself but in everyone around you as well (Matthew 12:35).

On those days when you can't seem to handle your temper or feel utterly insignificant in this world, take a walk outside and connect with God in nature.

Have you been there? Sometimes, does your anger get the best of you? It's incredible how being outside in nature can help you to calm down.

Harvest emphasizes that the seed is the basis for agriculture, the very foundation. Every tiny seed God creates is full of bio-grace and ensures the continuation of plants on the earth. God's power gives the seed life (1 Corinthians 3:6).

The life cycle of a plant begins with a tiny seed that contains DNA. Animals and humans also contain DNA.

Every plant has the essential body parts of seeds, flowers, or fruit. This provides the beginning process for circulating each specific type of plant on the earth, guaranteeing the next generation.

God tells the plant to prepare for freezing temperatures, dry weather, or a lack of water and nutrients to help with the dispersal of seeds with a process called dormancy. Instead of using energy to try to grow, the plant knows to conserve its energy until more conducive weather returns.

God has a very detailed plan for plants, but He loves you even more.

Just think of the plans He has for you! Have you asked Him what His plans are for you?

God has a plan for pine cones. They depend on fire's heat to break their seed's dormancy. The intense heat from a fire makes the seed's hard shell crack open, allowing water to do its job. The seed will then begin to grow, providing future pine trees.

Feeling the power of God's love is like that. The same mighty God that fills the sky with clouds, sends rain to the earth, and makes the grass grow on hills will lovingly come to live in your heart if you ask (Psalm 147:8).

Breaking through the dormancy of any anger or bitterness in your heart, His mighty spirit will saturate your life with awe, connecting and germinating the spiritual gifts He has gifted you.

Like you and me, size doesn't matter regarding the purpose God gives each seed. Orchid seeds are so tiny that they almost look like dust, yet they provide a fantastic flowering plant.

Coconuts have the largest seeds and can be classified as seeds, fruits, or nuts. The variations in the seeds' size help plants survive in their natural environments. Everything in nature works together perfectly, no matter what size.

Nature teaches that the purpose of life is a life of purpose. All aspects of nature work together beautifully to create and develop new life.

The Bible often talks about seeds, plants, and crops because we can all relate. In a parable, Jesus explained, "The kingdom of heaven is like a mustard seed that a man planted in his field. The mustard seed is very small but is one of the largest garden plants when it grows. It becomes big enough for the wild birds to come and build nests in its branches" (Matthew 13:31–32).

This helps explain that no one person is better than the other. Everyone's purpose is excellent.

The story teaches that even though the kingdom of God started small, when all believers connect to their God-given purpose, it will repetitively grow and spread across the earth to unlimited followers. When Jesus comes into your heart, He places His seed of life for all eternity.

"A morning glory at my window satisfies me more than the metaphysics of books" (Walt Whitman).

God created flowers to beautify the earth and provide enjoyment. Flowers also help protect the environment.

Flowers are not only colorful and smell good but are also very important to the plant. A flower attracts insects, such as bees, that feed on the flower's nectar. As the bees move from flower to flower, pollen sticks to their feet, and they help to pollinate or fertilize the plants. After fertilization, the flower develops into a fruit containing a seed.

If God had not created sunflowers, Vincent Van Gogh would not have been able to use the magnificent flowers as a subject to paint and show his faith. The gold and brown colors of the sunflowers are stunning in Vincent's artwork and symbolize his beloved creator.

As the son of a minister, Vincent Van Gogh had a Christian upbringing. He dealt with many struggles in life, searching for his purpose. God created Vincent and gifted him with a seed of incredible artistic talents. Vincent used the extraordinary talents God gave him to the best of his ability, reflecting his faith by painting the beautiful nature that God designed.

Try picking a bouquet of beautiful flowers, God's little friends, and placing them in a vase on your table. They are a lovely little reminder of God's precious love for you. Your heavenly Father makes His ever-loving presence simple to see if you are intentional and willing to see it.

"Just as a forest is not only trees, a grassland is not only grass. It is hundreds, literally hundreds of species of plants woven together in a complex fabric of interdependence" (Richard Manning, *Grassland: The History, Biology, Politics, and Promise of the American Prairie*, 1995).

A mixture of plants working together is always better than one kind by itself. An open prairie with many exquisite wildflowers, such as the Flint Hills of Kansas, exemplifies God-designed connectedness. Land that has never been broken, completely untouched by human hands, is God's nature at its finest (Psalm 23:1–2).

When God created, He designed with diversity. He made people, animals, and plants with distinctive shapes, sizes, and colors.

Being different can be such a beautiful thing. However, those variances can also divide us. Friends, we have an enemy, but it is not each other (Ephesians 6:12).

God simply asks for faith. People create religions, traditions, and gender categories to separate themselves, making their relationship with God complex.

When Jesus's followers came to Him inquiring if He knew that the Pharisees were mad at Him, He answered, "Every plant that my Father in heaven has not planted himself will be pulled up by the roots" (Matthew 15:13).

Three environmental conditions—the soil's temperature, moisture, and sunshine—are needed and must work together to regulate seed germination. How deep the seed is planted in the soil will also affect germination, alerting the seed to grow.

It takes many of nature's systems working together for the seed to grow when it is placed in the soil accurately. God created and collaborated the living systems of people, animals, and plants to work together correctly when we trust God's guidance.

Not all leaders choose to follow God's truth. God's designed creation is all about bringing people together to help share, show, teach, and learn from each other's differences.

Farming, conservation, and life are not an all-or-nothing, all-about-me kind of process. They have more of a give-and-take purpose. I will help you, and you help me.

Cooperation in nature is much more important than competition for everyone involved. God's creations are meant to accomplish a process with a purpose by working together.

Farmers have learned that as plant roots mature and grow deeper, they aerate the soil, providing an ideal germination-ready seedbed. God made plant roots to provide exudates.

When a plant needs something, it gives up energy to attract nutrients, causing soil particles to stick together like glue. The process plants repetitively provide is an energy source to create healthy soil in your garden.

God connects the designed purpose of plants and soil, benefiting each other. The world under our feet is very complex but well organized.

Regenerative farmers understand that the purpose of a living root repetitively provides answers to the process of farming and gardening.

God made plants with the very efficient purpose of creating their food and energy. Using the mystical and dynamic process of photosynthesis, during the day, a plant will connect with sunlight as the energy source, take in CO_2 from the air, and bring up water from the roots to create sugar and help the plant grow.

You might begin your day by connecting to the brewed beverage made from the roasted beans of the coffee plant. Some might start the day by consuming juice created from the fruit of an orange tree.

God designed plants to be a repetitive part of our lives daily, making His presence continually available. Have you ever thought about that? Do you recognize God's presence with every cup of coffee you drink and connect with Him?

"God said, 'Look, I have given you all the plants that have grain for seeds and all the trees whose fruits have seeds in them. They will be food for you. I have given all the green plants as food for every wild animal, every bird of the air, and every small crawling animal.' And it happened" (Genesis 1:29–30).

Grains such as rice, wheat, corn, and milo are seeds we use for food. Nuts are seeds we can eat or plant to grow a tree.

You are what you eat. God knows what your body needs because He created it. God continues to produce and offer plants that provide nutrients for your body.

Learning to grow your own food can be a great family activity. We need to teach the next generation to eat more whole foods, such as fruits and vegetables, instead of processed foods.

Some vegetables and fruits are shaped to look like the body part that they help. Sliced carrots resemble the pupil and iris of the eyes, tomatoes bear a resemblance to the heart in color and have four chambers, grapes look like the lungs' alveoli, and walnuts resemble a brain.

Nature provides a subtle hint of some of the benefits of specific God-given foods.

God designed plant diversity to increase microbial diversity. My farmer husband, along with many other farmers around the world, consistently grows cover crops.

Cover crops are a mixture of many plants grown to cover and benefit the soil rather than for the exclusive purpose of only being harvested.

Diverse plant communities keep plants healthier. Cover crops can begin to heal the soil people have messed up with tillage and other practices, manage insects, and control weeds.

Farmers and gardeners really don't control weeds; at best, they try to manage them. Weed populations change as the soil shifts, caused by the loss of vital components.

What happens to cause the change? Some farmers are testing the weeds with their crops to determine their nitrogen levels, helping to manage the crop.

"A weed is still a plant, but we don't understand its function completely" (Ray Archuletta).

I wish I could say that I am responsible for growing vegetables in my garden, but if I am honest, basically, all I do is watch. I am married to a farmer who grows crops on many acres, but sadly, his green thumb has not rubbed off on me.

I try to remember to water the plants and pull the weeds, but I get busy and forget. This tends to happen not only with my tomato plants but also in my spiritual life. Can you relate?

Do you let the weeds of life consume you by constantly

complaining, demanding answers, or accusing God of causing the problem? I would be lying if I said I had not done all these things at some point.

How do you talk to God when things aren't going your way? Maybe you got laid off, finances are tight, or you lost a loved one. But God can use the weeds to help you grow and become stronger.

"Then the Lord said to Job, 'Do you still want to argue with the Almighty? You are God's critic, but do you have the answers'" (Job 40:2).

Our response to personal struggles shows our attitude toward God. Remember, God loves you and has authority and power over everything.

Tell God why you are angry with Him and what you fear. He can take it. Chop down and pull out the weeds rather than becoming angry or resentful of God by letting weeds take over.

No matter what the circumstances, continue to trust Him. God will give you grace abundant enough even to love yourself and others.

God offers seeds of grace during times of disappointment. Your attitude toward your past, present, and future will determine where you plant your trust. He will listen to your prayers and provide wisdom to help you in your weedy situation.

Maybe you can try sharing your harvested seeds of grace with others, helping them to believe. Admit your fears and explain the process that helped you to overcome them. Explain to others how they can see God's presence in nature beside them daily, just like you do.

Plants must be rooted deep in rich soil to grow the beautiful flowers you see above the ground. Roots don't drink one day and decide the next that they don't need any more nourishment.

They are in it for the long haul.

Like a plant's roots, you know you must be continually rooted and connected to Jesus to grow and produce fruit from your spirit. To grow solid roots, you need healthy soil, light, and water that only He can provide.

Where do you put your roots down?

The Word of God is healthy soil for the person who hears, understands, accepts, and holds its truth in their heart (Isaiah 40:8). Jesus is the light and the only one who can provide living water.

Be sure to repetitively connect your roots deep in the refreshing water of Jesus (Jeremiah 17:8).

Your heavenly father has created a sanctuary of greenery on the earth for you to see and feel His love without fear. Place your hand on the rough bark of a strong tree, connect with God, and believe. God isn't the tree, but He created every fine detail of that amazing plant to remind you of His presence and show His nearness and love for you.

What are you afraid of? Give those fears to God.

Pick an apple, sit down, lean against the tree, and tell your heavenly Father what you are struggling with. Holding an apple is like holding God's hand; it shows God's presence.

As you munch on the fruit, feel the warm sunshine on your skin while you close your eyes and listen to the leaves clapping their hands in the wind. Your faith will grow as you know and believe that your heavenly Father, the Almighty Creator, crafted that apple just for you.

God created plants to remind you of Him.

Points to Ponder

Do people and animals have anything in common?

CHAPTER 12

ANIMALS ILLUMINATE THEIR CREATOR

Animal design days must have been some of God's favorite days in His creation week. I can't even imagine all the creative juices working in His mind to contemplate the numerous distinctive sizes, shapes, colors, and species of animals God made. How did He conceive so many unique, memorable, and unusual animals? He made each with a different purpose for living on this planet.

On the fifth day of creation week, God said, "Let the water be filled with living things, and let the birds fly in the air above the earth" (Genesis 1:20). Then God went to work creating every living thing that moves in the sea and every bird that flies, giving each one the ability to produce more of its own kind (Genesis 1:21–22).

On the sixth day, God said, "Let the earth be filled with animals, each producing more of its own kind. Let there be tame animals and small crawling animals and wild animals and let each produce more of its own kind. And it happened" (Genesis 1:24).

Animals vary drastically in shape, size, and appearance. However, even though a giraffe looks significantly different from a chicken, they are much the same yet distinct.

God made animals to have the same gut microbes as healthy soil. This makes complete sense if you think about it. "From the ground, God formed every wild animal and every bird in the sky" (Genesis 2:19a).

God created both wild and tame animals with a purpose. Beavers are in the wild to help regulate the ecosystem of the rivers. Bees pollinate 30 percent of the world's crops and 90 percent of the wild plants, explains GlobalGiving.org.

Domestic animals, such as the llama, guard other farm animals. Dogs can help rescue, guide, and emotionally support other animals and humans.

The Creator Himself takes care of the animals daily (Psalm 147:9). From a farm girl's perspective, I can't even imagine the list of chores God has each day. Would you want to take care of God's chores if He went on vacation?

Our heavenly Father ensures that the sea has just the right amount of saltiness for all the beautiful fish and sea animals, that wild animals and birds are fed, that seeds are growing to make more plants, and that flowers are blooming perfectly to feed insects.

God designed and continues to maintain the entire universe. Every day, all day, He takes care of you and me. No wonder He doesn't sleep (Psalm 121:1).

The "Great I Am" continually cares for the animals He creates. How cool is that? God is actively a part of their daily lives and yours (Psalm 50:10–11). You and I get to witness those unique partnerships to help us believe.

"Look at the birds in the air. They don't plant or harvest or store food in barns, but your heavenly Father feeds them.

And you know that you are worth much more than the birds. You cannot add any time to your life by worrying about it" (Matthew 6:26–27).

Do you consider the birds you see almost daily to be miracles? Think about the life of a bird. A male and female bird hang out together. The female lays her eggs. She keeps them at just the right temperature for babies to grow and mature. Babies develop knowing the exact time to peck themselves out and enter the world.

How do birds learn what to do in each step of their life? How do they know when to use their new wings? Who tells them when is precisely the right time to fly? God guides the animals just like you and me.

Animals don't have calendars; instead, they watch nature. Animals and plants focus on changes in light affecting the length of day and night. They don't need to follow daylight savings time; God gave them a sense of their own to observe nature.

The sun gives animals hints about the upcoming change of seasons.

- When days grow shorter and temperatures drop, animals like geese migrate south.
- Squirrels begin the process of storing food to get ready for winter.
- Bears adapt by growing thicker fur and hibernating.
- As days get longer and springtime comes, birds know to build nests in preparation to lay their colorful eggs.

God gifted animals with the ability to produce more of their own kind. Some animals are designed to accomplish this by laying eggs to hatch out their young, while others give birth to live babies.

Have you ever pondered how amazing it is that certain

animals can produce eggs? What an amazing gift God gave animals. Owls, turtles, ducks, snakes, chickens, alligators, and fish are just a few examples of animals that lay eggs to reproduce.

The increasing daylight and warmer temperatures in the spring are essential for triggering the God-given motherhood hormones. These hormones tell the female to find a mate, lay eggs, protect them, and keep them warm so that the eggs can hatch some babies.

The egg's design is a wonder of nature. God created the egg to exit the animal with its own packaging.

The American Egg Board has dubbed the chicken egg ad the "Incredible Edible Egg," with good reason.

Eggs are one of nature's most nutrient-dense foods, containing all nine essential amino acids the human body cannot make alone. If fertilized, the egg has the purpose of creating a new baby. Otherwise, it is breakfast. Some say a breakfast without eggs is hardly a breakfast at all.

Can you imagine life without eggs? Nope. Me either.

God made eggs to vary in size, weight, and density of the shell depending on the animal's size. A-Z-animals.com explains that the ostrich egg is the largest of all bird eggs. Each egg weighs around three pounds, making it about the weight of twenty-four chicken eggs.

The hummingbird egg is the smallest bird egg, the size of a pea.

Eggs are used for cooking, holiday decorating, and games. Easter egg hunts are a custom believed to have started in sixteenth-century Germany. Dr. Martin Luther organized egg hunts for his church's congregation.

The men would hide the eggs, allowing the women and children to search for them. This acknowledges the resurrection story of women being the first to find the empty tomb where Jesus's body had been placed.

Eggs represent resurrection and new life for believers. God made the outside of an egg appear cold and hard, yet new life can flourish from within. The grave keeps life locked in; eggs remind you of the tomb from which Jesus arose.

Like a chick hatching from an egg, Jesus came out of the grave. So from now on, every time you crack open an egg, think of the new life that Jesus provides for you.

God designed some species of animals to reproduce by birthing live offspring. The amount of time it takes for the baby to develop in the uterus depends on the type of animal.

- The gestation of the rabbit is thirty-one days.
- The gestation of the pig is 114 days.
- The gestation of the monkey is six months.
- The elephant is pregnant twenty-two months before the baby is born.

We know that by penning a bull (male) and a cow (female) together, they will connect and mate to create a baby. The baby grows in the momma cow for nine months. God provides bio-grace to make the miracle of a live baby calf being born.

Ranchers calculate when the gestation period will end to be prepared. Then they watch and wait to assist the cow if needed so the delivery goes well. God gifts the baby calf knowledge to survive.

The live birth of a baby animal is miraculous. After spending nine months in its mother's belly, a baby calf moves around minutes after being born, trying to stand up, walk, and nurse off its mom.

Somehow, it knows how and where to find nourishment the minute it is born. Only God could assist with this by providing much bio-grace. It is an absolute miracle to see that I never get tired of watching (Malachi 4:2).

God cares for the animals and has given them an innate ability to do things. Have you ever wondered why some animals automatically know how to swim?

God has a big world to oversee. He doesn't have time to hold floater and beginner swim classes for cows, horses, and dogs to teach them to swim. God gave animals abilities and skills to help them survive.

God designed animals to be absolutely amazing when He created them. Scientists study all aspects of animals and nature, trying to copy their designs. Bioinspiration is technology inspired by nature.

Science mimics nature in a process called biomimicry. DigitalTrends.com reveals that scientists study termites to design ventilation systems and model wind turbines after humpback whales. Japanese engineers studied the beak of the kingfisher bird to upgrade their speed bullet trains.

God created animals with different living cycles or routines that they follow.

- Geese and salmon migrate each year on a seasonal basis.
- Bats, bears, and bumblebees hibernate and sleep through the winter.
- Caterpillars go through metamorphosis, transforming into butterflies.
- Some animals live in water, and some walk on land.
- Some animals sleep during the day, and some sleep at night.

God created each type of animal with a specific purpose, just like you and me. Animals repetitively connect and work together, helping each other out.

After Uncle Roger's accident, my dad milked the cows and did chores on my uncle's farm for several weeks before the dairy disbursement sale. I would ride with Dad to my cousin's farm whenever I could to hang out.

Dad assigned Les and me a few chores with specific instructions to stay out of trouble until the evening milking was finished. Then we fed the baby calves.

Gathering eggs and taking care of the chickens was on our list. Chickens are funny animals. They follow you around curiously, moving their head back and forth, watching your every move while singing their little song.

Nesting boxes are dark and have no lights. Critters can hide in a chicken house—snakes, raccoons, you name it. The unknown of searching with your hand in a dark space for eggs is scary.

Old hens lay eggs and never move. They have sharp beaks. Try to take their eggs, and they will use their beaks against you.

It was getting dark when Les strolled into the dusty, feather-infested chicken house. He was ecstatic to see a big, fat gray opossum. Hearing us, it waddled toward the corner, trying to get away.

A typical farm boy, Les was drawn to the opossum like a moth to a flame. Instantly, he located a long wooden stick underneath to check for babies.

Sticking my head in the smelly chicken house, I hollered to leave it alone as he continued to mess with the overgrown rat. As I yelled something about the possibility of it biting him, I watched the opossum leap forward and lock her jaw onto Les's pant leg.

In all my days, I had never seen an opossum do that!

Les let out a high-pitched shriek and began screaming like a little girl. Jumping and dancing around, he tried to shake the overgrown rat from his leg. With my feet in high gear, I faintly heard Les yelling to get Uncle Gary as I ran to the barn.

The milk barn is a quiet and somber place. The only noises are the humming of the milk machines and an old radio playing classic country. Cows need to be very calm and tranquil to let their milk down.

Kids are not welcome when cows are in the milk barn. I tried concentrating on this important fact as I frantically raced toward the barn.

On a covert mission, I slid through the hallowed doorway into the milking parlor. Immediately, I saw the disapproval on the faces of the adults milking in the pit. The second Dad laid eyes on me, he motioned for me to leave.

I shook my head from side to side, franticly waving for him to come to me. Les needed help, and I was not leaving the barn without Dad (Proverbs 13:13).

Dad was ignoring my version of sign language. I crept over to the stairs of the pit and quietly told him about Les. I tried to whisper, but the more I explained, the more excitement seemed to spill out. I can hardly talk without my hands anyway.

Every cow in the parlor was trying to crank her head around to locate the source of the noise. Not an easy task for a 1,100-pound cow standing in a milk stall.

The massive black-and-white bovine beside me did not appreciate my enthusiasm and began dancing around. Dad was not happy with me. With a few big steps, he swiftly removed me from the barn (Proverbs 13:24).

Outside, Dad began lecturing me why I should not be in the milk barn. I emphatically interrupted, explaining that Les had a big hairy opossum on his leg and needed help! We need to hurry!

Dad was at a slow simmer by this point. Finally realizing

what I was trying to tell him, he grabbed a shovel and stomped off toward the chicken house with me close behind on his heels.

Les was still hopping around in the chicken house, yelling, "Get it off!" Dad quickly removed the opossum from Les's leg and the chicken pen. Then we received a stern life lesson speech.

Did you ever get those talks when you were young? You know, the talk that outlined responsibility, using your heads, and leaving wild animals alone. Les was always getting me in trouble (Proverbs 18:17).

Dad marched back to the barn to finish milking. I could see his mouth moving the whole way. He wasn't a singer, so I figured he must be talking to himself (Proverbs 13:1).

Back in the house, I recapped the entire chicken house incident for Les. Picturing him with that overgrown rat on his leg was the funniest thing ever.

It cracked me up just thinking about it. Les finally appreciated the humor and joined me. We laughed until we could hardly breathe.

God knew we needed some time off from our new reality of missing a family member. We were two young farm kids with huge life issues who needed a break.

It felt like we were frantically swimming to the surface to gasp for air. Filling our lungs with oxygenated laughter was comfortable and felt so good. My heart longed to be in a happy place again.

Laughing together was as close as we had been to our old normal in a long time. Uncle Roger's accident had changed everything.

The laughter seemed to summon the healing process of our hearts and souls. Our hearts longed for laughter to release the settled pain and sorrow. God knew we were hurting and could feel the heaviness.

God must have a sense of humor. Knowing the outcome, the Creator placed the fat, hairy opossum in the smelly, feather-invested chicken coop.

It was God's plan. God knew Les's weakness because God gave it to him. He created that young farm boy.

God knows you better than you know yourself. Being in the right place at the right time is why that hairy opossum was created.

The overgrown rat gave us a moment of glorious joy and relief from our shattered new reality. God knows what you need and exactly when you need it. Sometimes life is hard, but His timing is always perfect.

You and I like to think we are in charge, but that is far from the truth. God handles all the details of managing the universe and the opossums.

Things are going on, secrets of nature, that we will never understand. God repetitively continues to create and maintain the process and purpose of this amazing earth that He designed.

In chapter 39, God asks Job several questions about the lives and actions of various animals to demonstrate how limited Job's knowledge of nature is. God is not expecting any answers; instead, He is trying to make a point.

God wanted Job to change his perspective, to acknowledge and surrender to God's power and sovereignty instead of relying on his own. Only by adjusting his thoughts could Job understand what God was really trying to tell him.

God used Job's lack of knowledge regarding the earth's natural order and animals to reveal his inability to understand God's moral order. Job was a simple human being. He did not have the ability or the right to judge the God who created the universe by asking why bad things were happening to him.

If nature is beyond Job's grasp of understanding, how could

he possibly comprehend God's mind and character?

God is God, and there is no other. When God asks you questions, they are not for His benefit. God already knows the best solution.

Inquiries from the Almighty Creator are His way of helping you see the situation openly and honestly, examining the role you play in His plan.

God knows your true feelings and will help you deal with them to release your fears. Let go of your past hurts. Give God a chance to reveal His greater purpose for you.

How cool is it to watch animals interact with each other? Animals communicate to show emotions and experience good and bad days. They make sounds and gestures, communicating just like people do. I would love to understand their language and listen to some of their conversations.

God's plan involves a process of seasons that unfold during your life, probably not at the exact moment you desire. Repetitively connecting with and leaning on God will help you grow and mature in your relationship with Him.

"But ask the animals, and they will teach you, or ask the birds of the air, and they will tell you. Speak to the earth, and it will teach you, or let the fish of the sea tell you. Every one of these knows that the hand of the Lord has done this. The life of every creature and the breath of all people are in God's hand"(Job 12:7–10).

Working with animals and caring for them daily helped me realize at a young age that animals and people are not very different. Animals share personalities and mood swings just like people.

God made hamsters, giraffes, hippos, and many other animals to have unique personalities. Your dog will never wake up some morning and decide he's mad and doesn't love you anymore. However, cats seem to have a different outlook on life.

The Bible uses animals in many parables and stories. When God created Balaam's donkey, He knew He would gift the donkey to speak. God allowed Balaam's donkey to express his thoughts as he saw the angel of the Lord standing on the road.

"Then the LORD made the donkey talk, and she said to Balaam, 'What have I done to make you hit me three times?'" (Numbers 22:28–30).

Jesus taught faith and peace to His disciples by displaying His power over nature (Matthew 21:18–22). God used wild and tame animals as examples in scripture (Matthew 10:16, 8:20; Isaiah 60:8).

I think animals show God's tender, loving heart. People who take care of animals possess a big heart. They learn to read the animals' wants and needs, as parents care for their kids, and our heavenly Father cares for us.

God created animals for us to enjoy as pets and friends. They are meant as companions but not to replace relationships with people (Matthew 12:11–12).

When my daughter left for college, her miniature dachshund stayed home with us. I enjoyed Snickers and was his caretaker for several years until he passed. It wasn't until after he was gone that I realized how much of my time and effort Snickers encompassed.

I considered getting another dog, but then I realized I always thought about Snickers needing water, food, or a potty break during the day. He was consuming a lot of my time.

What if I had spent that same amount of time and money blessing others and sharing Jesus? What could I have accomplished? Have you ever considered how many hours and dollars each week you spend caring for your pets? It might be eye-opening.

Working with animals and taking care of pets is a big responsibility. Bad situations can happen if you don't know what you are doing.

Let me tell you about Donna, a young, newly married bride. Even though she was a city girl, she was eager to help her new husband's family work cattle. Donna didn't know where to stand or what to do, so she tried not to get in the way.

Her plan worked until the large herd of cattle spooked and began running toward her. Donna knew she could not outrun them and froze.

A voice interrupted her frantic thoughts and repeatedly told her to stand still like a tree: "Keep your arms at your sides and be still."

As the stampede of cattle rumbled closer, Donna could feel the ground begin to shake. She closed her eyes, desperately focusing on trying not to be fearful and remain still like a tree. Between the dust, low bellowing, and frequent brushes of cattle hides rubbing against her arms, the herd thundered around her.

After the herd of cattle passed, Donna wiped the dirt from her face as she opened her eyes. Gratefully, she walked forward out of the cloud of dust, completely unharmed.

Her new husband and family watched the entire scene in horror. All were utterly shocked and amazed to see her walking toward them.

The family praised God, for they knew she was alive only by the mighty hand of the Almighty Creator.

Just like God has a plan for animals, He also has a plan and purpose for you and me. I know this personally because Donna is my mother.

I would not be writing this if the Almighty Creator had not miraculously saved my mom that day. Because God creates,

He repetitively plans and communicates with all living things. God tells the animals how to do what they do.

Like people, dairy cows, horses, and many other animal species have a social or pecking order. They respect their elders.

When it was time to milk, the cows waited in a big pen behind the barn, all mixed up and freely walking wherever they wanted. The cows entered the barn in pretty much the same order each day.

The older cows are in charge. The younger cows follow their orders for the most part. Occasionally, you might see a younger cow trying to sneak in and show some attitude, but an older cow will soon put her in her place. Animals don't create their own plan but are obedient to their Creator.

I think the horse must be one of God's favorite animals. Many references in the Bible relate to the horse and its social place in history. Revelations describe different colors of horses, symbolizing events that will occur during the tribulation.

Throughout history, horses signified the worldly power of Egypt and its armies.

- Haman had his ideas about how the king should honor a man who involved a horse (Esther 6:8).

- God gave Elijah the speed to run ahead of Ahab's horse and chariot (1 King 18:46).

- David first established a force of cavalry and chariots (2 Samuel 8:4).

- Solomon had 40,000 stalls of horses for his chariots and 12,000 men to ride them (1 King 4:26).

Kings rode horses and stallions that were strong and muscular. The rider must hold the reins of a stallion tightly, constantly pulling back to retain control. The animal will continually sidestep and prance around while fighting the rider's authority.

Jesus entered Jerusalem on the first Palm Sunday humbly and in peace. People could interact with Him. Jesus was probably using only a loose rope halter on the donkey, with nothing in its mouth. He could lay the reins on the donkey's neck as it diligently and reverently carried Jesus along the trail.

Jesus was royalty, but if He had ridden into Jerusalem on a strong, muscular stallion, it would have changed the crowd's focus. People placing coats and palm branches before Him could have possibly been harmed or trampled. The stallion would have commanded the attention of the crowd.

Jesus was riding on a donkey that had never been ridden (Mark 11:2). A colt is male, and a foal is less than a year old. Even though it had never been ridden, the donkey did not buck or throw a fit.

Friend, if you or I had tried to ride that young, unbroke donkey, we would have probably been left lying on the ground.

Donkeys are thought of as lowly, doing only menial labor. The donkey knew carrying Jesus through the streets that day was an honor.

Jesus greeted the crowd as He journeyed down the path to the temple. Standing proudly, the young donkey performed his job faithfully, like a stallion going to war. We should all have childlike faith like the young donkey.

The donkey is the only animal born with a cross on its back. Jesus the Messiah rode into Jerusalem on a cross and left Jerusalem with a cross (Matthew 12:40). The young donkey proudly served his master.

God designed and created each amazing animal and continues to care for you and them daily. Believe in Him. Step out of your box and look at the big picture. God's presence goes with you wherever you want to see Him (Psalm 36:7).

God gifted birds with exceptional abilities. They travel and play in the wind and the sky.

Are you intentional and aware when outside in nature? Do you pay attention and look for God? Step out in faith and depend on the Almighty Creator to live the life He designed explicitly for you.

Take a walk outside and watch the birds as they soar. They can glide in the air, swooping up and down seamlessly. Birds are a God thing.

Hope comes with knowing God has a plan; don't miss out on all God has in store for you. Don't let fear take control, causing you to miss seeing the fantastic animals He created.

If you look, you will see God continually right where you are (Matthew 10:29–31).

Points to Ponder

What do you think God looks like?

CHAPTER 13

GOD CREATED PEOPLE

*G*od made you and me to look like Him, naming us human beings (Genesis 5:2).

People are born either male or female. Men can sit side by side, and their shoulders touch. Women sit side by side, and their hips touch. Can you relate?

God formed each of us for the unique jobs we are assigned to do.

The highlight of God's creation week must be day six. All morning long, God worked hard to create animals of different shapes, sizes, and colors. Once He finished the animals, the Almighty Creator formed His most prized handiwork.

After lunch, God began to express His true joy and love (Genesis 1:26). He outdid Himself, crafting people in His likeness and image.

Step by step, God developed one living creation and then the next using a pattern. Each day God created living things, His creations became more complex (Psalm 139:1).

Can you see how God created with a purpose and plan to help you believe? Can you visualize how He connected many natural processes into a particular order?

God blessed humans, saying, "Have many children and grow in number. Fill the earth and be its master. Rule over the fish in the sea, the birds in the sky, and every living thing that moves on the earth" (Genesis 1:28).

God designed plants, animals, and people to have many things in common yet significant differences. Science. howstuffworks.com explains that every living thing consists of similar microscopic units called cells. These are the basic building blocks of life for plants, animals, and humans.

Plant cells have chloroplasts, while animal and human cells do not. According to Pediaa.com, the main difference between animal and human cells is the size and composition of the genome.

Animal cells have a different genome size for each species and can be reptiles, insects, or amphibians. Human cells repetitively have the same genome of three billion base pairs and can only make humans.

God designed animals and humans with many of the same essential body parts. Animals and humans (with some exceptions) have eyes, ears, a mouth, nose, teeth, hair, arms, legs, and personalities. Many internal organs, such as the heart, lungs, liver, blood, skin, bones, and muscles, are the same for mice to cows.

You are formed from the same basic pattern as animals, with a few upgrades. Have you ever considered that?

- Your organ systems, such as the respiratory, cardiovascular, and nervous systems, are similar to those of animals. Humans can function with organs transplanted from animals.

- Animals and people become ill with some of the same diseases, called zoonotic sicknesses. Each species has physical similarities and differences.

- Plants, animals, and you use oxygen, water, sunlight, carbon dioxide, and food. All require rest to produce energy for their bodies to work correctly.

- God made animals and humans from healthy soil.

- God formed humans from healthy soil with much love by using His hands. God spoke creation into place by faith, not by works.

When God created people, He made them in His image. This separates humans from all other created beings and establishes a unique bond with our Creator.

God created you and me to connect personally with Him. You are the ultimate of all creation, repetitively reflecting your heavenly Father's goodness and glory. God lovingly took the time to mold healthy soil into His future children and family.

Does that make you feel special? You are the cherry on top of all creation. God loves you that much.

God lovingly came down to earth and got dirty. Manually creating, God formed His magnum opus called Adam out of the dust. God blew His breath of life into Adam for life.

Your heavenly Father created you in the same way that He wants you to approach Him. He set the bar high, creating a fundamental example.

God knew being alone was not good for His new friend, Adam. He wanted to find Adam a helper and companion (Genesis 2:18). So God brought all the animals to Adam to be named.

Can you even imagine fulfilling such a daunting task? How did Adam think of so many different names?

After naming all the animals, Adam still did not find a suitable partner to help multiply and fill the earth. God knew what Adam needed in a companion, and I think He wanted Adam to see that he could not find one on his own.

So God caused Adam to sleep deeply. God removed a rib and used it to create Adam's soulmate. Adam called her woman because she was taken out of man (Genesis 2:23).

God lovingly used His hands to create a partner for Adam. She is the mother of every human who has ever lived, so Adam named her Eve.

"But in the Lord women are not independent of men, and men are not independent of women. This is true because woman came from man, but also man is born from woman. But everything comes from God" (1 Corinthians 11:12).

The Almighty Creator knows who you are and everything about you. God made the process of His relationship with people personal by taking the time and effort to form Adam and Eve with His own hands (James 1:8). You are an excellent visual sensation made with foresight.

Michelangelo worked on many projects with vision and is well-known as an extremely talented painter, sculptor, and artist. I can barely draw stick people.

I really don't relate to Michelangelo's focus on working night and day with a mental picture of a massive block of marble. But I can relate to his passion as a mother.

God provides grace to humans in so many ways. We fall in love, get married, then decide we want a little one.

You are so excited when you find out you are pregnant and carrying a baby. Then reality sets in, and the perfect Norman Rockwell picture of a baby in your arms gets a little blurry.

The troubles of creating a work of art begin to surface. You might puke in the morning or all day. You might not feel so good and always seem to be tired. Friend, there is nothing like a pregnant tired. But you welcome the work because you are focused and know in your heart and soul that you and God are in the process of creating a masterpiece.

Humans experience the fun process of putting the male and female together, and God takes over and does all the work. He knows what your sweet baby will look like even before you plan to get pregnant.

God decides the DNA to use for eye color, straight or curly hair, and how tall or skinny your sweet baby will grow up to be. God knows exactly what your baby will look like, providing the process of bio-grace to make it happen.

As your watermelon stomach continually swells, you proudly carry the veiled creation. A wise woman once told me that God would have made your belly button a window if he had wanted you to see the gender.

In the last few weeks, you have always been tired, your back hurts, you can't sleep at night, and comfort seems impossible. There are hours of pain while delivering the baby, but finally, you get to hold your sweet, new, perfectly sculptured masterpiece. Mommy, Daddy, and God physically created a beautiful human being.

Every human begins with the same process. According to TheWorldCounts.com, 4.5 babies are born somewhere in the world every second of the day.

Created in your mother's womb, God created you specifically. You are a masterful work of God, visualized and made on purpose (Isaiah 40:11).

Genesis 1:26 tells us that people are created in God's image, but what does that mean exactly? Do you look like Him?

I have always wondered how much we look like our heavenly Father. What color is His hair, or does He still have any? Maybe you have your heavenly Father's nose or eye color.

Adam and Eve walked with God in the garden. He must

not have looked scary, or they would have run away, right? How cool it must have been for God to be your walking buddy.

After God finished creating on the sixth day, He probably stood up and stretched. Brushing the extra dust from His clothes, He might have taken a step backward. After viewing His masterpiece, He probably leaned closer to tweak His work while adjusting the fine details.

I imagine God leaning against a tree, drinking a cold glass of water while looking over everything He had made that day. Even though He was tired, He was grinning from ear to ear, knowing His work was exceptional.

Crossing His arms over his chest, maybe He tipped his head a little to the side to help Him think like I do. Perhaps He pondered if He should have sculpted the right arm a little rounder or the left leg a little longer. But after viewing His finished product for all to hear, He calmly said, "It was very good."

What? That's it? I mean, wow! What an understatement that is. God had just designed, engineered, and created a miraculous human being.

In his book *The Human Body*, Dr. Peter Abrahams states, "Akin to the most masterly machine, the human body is comprised of billions of microscopic units, each with their own unique function yet all working together to create one smoothly operating entity."

His book explains that the human body contains DNA, biorhythms, and working cells that divide and communicate. We have hair and nails that grow, skin, muscles, and blood that transport life-giving oxygen and vital nutrients to cells, allowing the body to function. The body has bones, nerves, kidneys, and hormones, can sleep, and has a heart.

You get the point. There are no words to describe how excellent God's design of the human body is, yet God was content with stating, "It is very good."

How incredibly humble God must be? He had just finished creating the heavens and the earth, hanging the heavenly lights in the sky. He formed land and water, created oceans, and designed plants. God made animal species of all sizes and colors. Saving the best for last, He made people the cherry on top of His week's work.

God was proud, content, and pleased with what He had created by simply stating, "It is very good." God's statement was not about boasting, extra attitude, or strutting His stuff.

That is one of the many reasons God is such a loving God. Your heavenly Father created you to have fellowship with Him (Isaiah 46:4). That is who He is—a loving and personable God. He wants you to connect with him and others. Love God. Love people.

Isn't that amazing? The Creator of everything cares about you and me! God chose you before all other world creations to be holy and blameless. Wow! That is such an honor.

Using a process with His hands, He created your body to be a recognizable work of art without a written signature. But inside, He placed a heart in which He can live.

God granted you gifts designed to enjoy the outdoors and connect with others. You are endowed with five senses to see, touch, taste, smell, and hear the incredible experience of nature. Sights, sounds, and smells all unite to provide experiences that remind you of places, people, and events.

What sights and sounds do you video to watch again later? What smells would you bottle up to share?

- The calming smell of fresh rain can be almost therapeutic.
- The smell of fresh soil can be like medicine for the soul.

The scent of rain right before a storm is not the rain itself.

The smell comes from moistening the ground.

Popular Science tells us that petrichor forms from plants and bacteria that live in the soil. Petrichor combines fragrant chemical compounds created from oils made by plants and actinobacteria. God designed the purpose of raindrops mixing with dry soil to create the amazing smell of rain.

A little girl named Danae sat on her mother's lap, chattering nonstop with others around her. On a hot afternoon in 1996 near their home in Irving, Texas, she suddenly fell silent as she hugged her arms across her chest. "Can you smell that?" she asked with much enthusiasm.

Smelling the air and detecting the approach of a thunderstorm, her mom stated that it smelled like rain. Caught in the moment, Danae shook her head and patted her thin shoulders with tiny hands. Then she loudly announced that it smelled like Him. Like God when you lay your head on His chest.

Danae was born prematurely, shares Truthorfiction.com. Her little body was too sensitive for anyone to touch. Her mother's eyes filled with tears as her daughter confirmed what she had felt in her heart all along. God had held Danae during those long days and nights of her first two months of life. God's loving scent during that time is what she remembers so well.

Your God-given senses help you recognize your surroundings and believe in the Almighty Creator. Your senses allow you to experience life on five different levels and beyond, something most healthy people simply take for granted.

God fashioned nature to arouse the purpose for each of your senses. You can taste the sweet nectar of a juicy, ripe peach in your mouth. At the same time, you are listening to the sounds of wind drifting slowly, effortlessly, through the leaves of the peach tree. Hearing the woosh of wind rattling the leaves helps you experience life while nurturing your body and soothing your mind.

Your eyes observe a flamboyant bird as it perches on a branch to sing melodiously. Prickly hairs covering the outside skin of the peach intrigue your tongue as sweet nectar fills your mouth. Your eyes adore the massive wildflower-filled meadow and watch them dance around the tree. You sense the sweet nectar of the peach as you sniff the aroma of the exquisite flowers. Gifts from God that bring peace to your mind and soul.

We tend to concentrate on things that only affect us directly. When you focus on God's presence in nature each day, can you thank Him in every situation, good or bad? Can you place your faith before your fear?

God initiated the building process of your senses from the moment you were created. He makes touch the strongest sensation when a baby is born.

Explains WhatToExpect.com, touch is the first sense to develop just three weeks after conception. All senses are established by week eight of gestation and fully functional before birth.

EveryDayHealth.com. shares the following:

- Humans can detect at least one trillion distinct scents.

- God gave women a better sense of smell than men.

- Dogs have nearly forty-four times more scent cells than humans.

- Like fingerprints, each human has their own distinct odor. Think about that the next time you meet someone.

God created nature at His command (Revelation 5:13). He designed nature and your senses to have an amazing connection, a partnership that works together for your enjoyment. Nature nourishes your body and soul, supplying a beautiful way to see God's presence daily.

Do you ever really think about God's plan for the earth and how He created it? Can you see how God's plan repetitively connects to you every minute of every day?

As children of God, we can also enjoy the natural freedom and relationship with the Creator we are born with. The peace of God will spontaneously saturate your soul.

Watching my granddaughter dance, I am reminded that we are born without fear of others' opinions. She freely dances peacefully, moving whatever part of her body she wants, enjoying the music in her little world as the melody touches her heart. There is no care in the world about what others think.

As you age, the fearful words of others can change your perspectives, tunneling your vision and causing you to look only for what is standing directly before your eyes.

Everything in God's creation is under His control. Using animals as examples for Job, God exposed it is foolish for people to think they can stand up against God when they are afraid to confront even a crocodile (Job 41:9). Your heavenly Father is all-powerful and will do what He knows is best, regardless of what you think is fair.

God's purpose and process do not depend on ours. God's questions to Job revealed that he was an imperfect human being.

God knows and is connected to the big picture because He is the author of life. Job could not judge the God who created the universe, nor did he have the right to ask why He does what He does.

Job's friends were convinced a great sin had caused his suffering. Be careful not to judge others because you don't know what God is doing. God is working in ways you know nothing about.

After receiving much criticism from his friends, Job still

prayed for them as God instructed him to do (Job 42:10). Forgiving someone who has accused you of wrongdoing is difficult, but Job did.

Are you praying for those who have hurt you? Can you forgive them? Following Job's example and praying for those who may have said bad things about you will provide peace.

God gave communication to every living thing in nature, a process we take for granted.

Dolphins, coconut trees, lizards, and stars exchange information to understand each other. Facial expressions, gestures, emotions, sounds, and body language are universal ways people, animals, and creation talk to each other, speaking volumes.

Even though we might be using the same communication techniques, we each have our own twist on the presentation. Cultural backgrounds, how we were raised, gender, and temperament all affect how communication is expressed.

Connecting the lives of every creature on earth creates relationships.

Every living creation wants to be understood. I talk to my horse, and he talks back to me. We don't speak the same verbal language, but I can figure out what he wants.

Successful communication can avoid conflicts and help connect us with better decision-making. Listening with love is one of the most essential aspects of exchanging ideas in any relationship. God gave people and animals two ears and only one mouth.

People and animals are not created to live life alone. We need each other. To have a friend, you must be a friend.

Think about your relationships with others. Put down your screen and listen to the people God has placed around you. Friends and family should have your best interest in mind.

Learning what matters most to you and others will change your world. Soak in knowledge from those who have lived life and invest in your people. Ponder the thoughts about yourself listed below.

- How much of your life are you willing to share?
- Did God create you to be strong-willed and independent, or is it your idea?
- Are you a gracious giver and receiver in friendships, or do you want to do it all yourself?
- How well do you observe nature? Do you look for what is behind, around, and near you?
- How will you follow God's direction for your life? What goals does He want you to accomplish?

What do you want God to look like? More importantly, what do you need God to look like? God is God, and He is the great I Am. You don't define Him; He defines you and your purpose.

Get to know your Creator. You are a complex creature of His conception.

God designed your soul to speak for you. Your body does not define who you are. God created you special because He longs to have an intimate heart relationship with you, His child (Psalm 103:13–15).

Starting a conversation with those around you is natural. When walking into a classroom for the first time, you look for a place to sit.

You will begin to get to know the people in the room and make new friends. The next time you come to class, you will feel more comfortable. If you don't speak or interact with others, you will remain unknown to them.

Your connection with God is similar. He will be unknown

to you until you speak to and have a relationship with your heavenly Father.

The pastor I listened to when I was growing up constantly spoke about the importance of reading the Bible and how God uses it to talk to each of us. After Uncle Roger's accident, I wondered if God still wanted to talk to me.

I assumed God probably didn't want anything to do with me if He could read my mind. But wondering what God would say got the best of me, so I read my Bible at home. Not knowing where to start, I began reading Genesis with plans to read the entire book.

Trying to read my King James Bible seemed impossible. The words seemed hard to pronounce and understand, as they went right over my head. How was I supposed to make any sense of this? No one talks using words like shall and ye. What is with all the lists of random names that go on forever?

I tried reading verses in different chapters of different books without success. My young mind could not comprehend and was overwhelmed. Disappointed, I gave up reading.

The Sunday school teacher announced she would award points for bringing my Bible to church. I figured at least I could win something since my parents made me attend church every week anyway, so my Bible went to church with me on Sundays.

I adored the new puffy sticker I received for bringing my white, zippered Bible to Sunday school. The sticker featured a bright green and yellow striped caterpillar with little googly eyes. "God's not finished with me yet" was written under the cute little creature.

I proudly stuck him front and center on my Bible. Every time my eyes would see the Bible, I read the phrase. I read it over and over, wondering exactly what it meant.

When God created you, He called you by name. You were

made in His image on purpose, for a purpose. You were formed to reflect God's love to a hurting world.

Each of us has a different calling, a mission to show the world what God's love looks like. Until your heart stops beating, God will never be finished with you. He longs for your heart to be wholly fixed on Him without fear.

The heart determines your body's physical life and is also involved in your spiritual life with God as well. Physically, your heart keeps your body alive. Your spirit leaves the body when the heart stops beating.

If Jesus lives in your heart when you die, He will take your spirit up to heaven to live with Him eternally. If you don't have a relationship with Jesus, your spirit will fall to hell. When Jesus is in your heart, He is with you in everything you experience forever.

Humans are blessed to have been gifted a heart to receive God's love (1 Corinthians 7:23).

- Thoughts from your heart shape you into who you will become (1 Corinthians 4:5).

- What you believe is stored in your heart (Proverbs 23:7).

- What you constantly think about matters. Your heart is where you keep your cherished thoughts.

The eyes speak of the heart and are physically connected to the body.

"Your heart is important to your eyes," explains Eyecare. org. God designed your eyes to have the highest oxygen consumption of any organ in the body. Oxygen for your eyes comes from the heart. Poor circulation due to heart disease can harm the function of the eyes and lead to vision loss or even blindness.

God gifted people with a consciousness that affects their

hearts. Animals do not have this. The coyote does not lie awake at night worrying about the family of the rabbit he just ate.

God specifically designed people to have a heart for Jesus and a soul that can spend eternity with Him.

Friend, you are where heaven and earth meet. Your body is a temple of God created to do the work He has purposely set aside for you.

Everyone is designed to be a temple of God (1 Corinthians 6:19–20). God's children allow God's spirit to lead them in fulfilling His plan for our families, churches, and the world (Ephesians 2:8–10).

Your body is a living temple and is not your own. It belongs to God, who created and purchased it with the precious and priceless blood of Jesus, His Son.

Wherever you go, whatever you experience, the Holy Spirit is also exposed to it. Chemical abuse, alcohol abuse, and your thoughts and words can all be offensive to the Holy Spirit. "God's temple is holy, and you are that temple" (1 Corinthians 3:17).

You are a part of God's plan and purpose for creation and will never be separated from Him. Never will He withdraw himself from what he asks you to do (Romans 8:1–11).

God hasn't ever divided His law from His presence. You are created by and belong to Jesus. Jesus belongs to God (1 Corinthians 3:23).

- Only God knows exactly why you do what you do. God truly understands you because He made you!

- Sometimes, human actions are too complex for other humans to understand. Can you relate?

- Nothing you do will surprise God. You are a cocktail of DNA that He mixed together.

God wants nothing more than your love and trust. You mean the world to God, and He continually creates everything for you. Only He knows what you actually need.

Walk outside, talk to God as your friend, and converse. Look for His presence in nature.

Praying isn't something you do to an unknown God. Search your heart and soul, invite God there, and you will search no more. There is no love as fulfilling as God's love.

You might not want to hang out with people as much once you experience the peace in God's creation that only He can provide. Solitude in nature with God is addictive.

God has loved you and had a plan for you since eternity began. Believe in the one true God.

Points to Ponder

How do you deal with change?

CHAPTER 14

THE PROCESS OF TIME

Do you see time as a challenge, an obstruction, or a gift? Everything in God's created universe revolves around His purpose of time. The life of each created being rests in God's perfect timing.

Since God created time and knows how it works, He is the only one who can change it.

The book of Joshua explains that as God was fighting for Israel, He allowed Joshua to ask that the sun's process stop. Nature recognizes and obeys its Almighty Creator and follows the command of His loving voice. The sun waited in the middle of the sky and did not go down for a full day (Joshua 10:13). This has never happened before or after that day.

Scientists actively ponder why time only moves forward. No physical evidence can support the idea that anything escapes from time, moves time backward, or pushes time forward, explains Space.com.

When you open your eyes each morning, do you recognize your many connections with God through the timing of nature's beautiful song?

Nature is designed for you to repetitively see the kingdom of God's presence not in His person but in power (1 Corinthians 4:19–20). God's power and strength are very great (Ephesians 1:19). From soil to sky, God creates everything above and below your feet, connecting you with His incredible, abundant, gracious, and timely process (Deuteronomy 10:14).

Does anything in your life ever remain the same? God designed everything about life to change continually.

Nothing remains the same because of the purpose of time (Ecclesiastes 3:11). The weather, tides, planted seeds, and everything living and breathing in creation are connected to time and change daily (2 Corinthians 5:17). Trees, animals, and people age with each sunset.

Can you see how nature is designed to help germinate your belief in the Almighty Creator (Proverbs 27:1)?

God's meticulous timing continually regulates all of creation (James 4:13–17). However, the process of time does not affect our heavenly Father.

God never changes (Malachi 3:6). His greatness is beyond the human mind (Psalm 145:3–5). God's characteristics remain constant, His promises will never fail, and His plans cannot be spoiled (Numbers 23:19). God existed before time began. He has no beginning, and He will have no end.

Jon Nielson explains, "God's aseity refers to God being eternally and completely 'of himself.'" God is from and of Himself, dependent on nothing else. However, you and I do not share this characteristic.

God is eternal (1 Timothy 1:17). God's knowledge, wisdom, and understanding are unlimited. There is no error at all in anything He does, says, or wills.

Everything God has written down and said will always be there without change (Jeremiah 1:12). God is actually outside the purpose and process of time that He created.

Snickers had been a member of our family for thirteen years. When I arrived home, I found his kennel door open. The miniature dachshund's eyesight and health were failing.

The weather was changing to cold wind and rain, and we desperately searched for him until way after dark. Our hearts ached, imagining that our sweet puppy dog might be chilly, scared, and outside alone.

The search began early the following day. My heart's voice told me to walk through the pasture behind the house and look along the creek bank. I obeyed and walked directly to where Snickers was lying.

My fears disappeared as soon as I saw our little dachshund. The sweet puppy dog was all stretched out, sunning himself, and looked like he was taking a serious nap.

He didn't have a care in this world when he left it. Lying in the sun on the thick green grass next to the creek, Snickers was surrounded by everything Psalm 23 describes.

Even though tears were rolling down my face, I could only smile and thank Jesus over and over for taking such excellent care of Snickers. God's timing was perfect. My college-aged daughter had been struggling to care for her aging canine friend.

As I walked back to the house, the song "Great Is Thy Faithfulness" played in my mind.

God is always working behind the scenes with His impeccable timing. Every aspect of nature connects to and highlights God's power. The only thing constant is change because the process of life was designed that way.

Do you ever think about the wind? Where does it even come from? How does it cause such incredible consequences when we only see its effects (John 3:8)?

Even though many secrets of nature are hidden, and we cannot see how they work, their purpose reflects God's power beyond anything we can fully comprehend or imagine. An apple is a great example.

You and I can open an apple and count the number of seeds inside. We know and expect that each one of those seeds can produce an apple tree. However, God is the only one who knows the possibility of how many apples are in each one of those seeds.

Job describes God's great power and mighty works in chapters 4–37 as he converses with his friends. Job tells of God's wisdom as He commands the sun not to shine (Job 9:7), moves mountains (Job 9:5), and has the life of every creature in His hand (Job 12:10).

God's powerful endeavors are many and great yet often hidden from our sight. Nature repetitively commands tremendous influence on the earth, happenings beyond anything we can fully comprehend or imagine. Nature is God.

How do all the different patterns occur in nature? How do your eyes and brain process images and information so intently? God designed, continues to create, and holds complete authority over the universe.

"No one has ever given me anything that I must pay back because everything under the sky belongs to me" (Job 41:11). God created everything, including your life (Ecclesiastes 7:14).

Beholding the raw Almighty hand of God as you hear the thunder roll across storm clouds or see a brightly colored rainbow after a rainstorm will give your heart hope, erasing fears as you hold onto the certainty of the future.

God's perfect timing and purpose are responsible for everything because He continually plans it. Believe and know that you can trust Him when He guides or instructs you because He is always right (Romans 11:33).

Your existence and timing are not arbitrary or by chance. I believe there is no such thing as coincidence.

We don't need to worry about or create future plans. God has the master plan, and it is timed out perfectly. Infinity makes it difficult for you and me to comprehend eternity without reference points. Our lack of understanding causes small thinking.

Everything in and about your life is a process of time. Dealing with time requires patience, logic, planning, and work.

Once you realize that living life is an orderly process of continual change, it will become much more acceptable and appreciated. Nothing worthwhile is instantaneous; if it is, you probably won't appreciate or treasure it as you should.

Making peace with change will allow you to be ready when you expect it (2 Corinthians 5:18). It will also change your relationship with time, becoming much more positive. This will help you spend your time wisely, as you realize it is a gift from God (James 1:17).

My friend and her young family moved into their first home during the winter months. Now that it was springtime, she excitedly explained that the ugly, dead plants beside the house they planned to remove were growing new leaves and had come to life. I briefly described a little about dormancy in plants.

God designed every vegetable, flower, and plant to have optimal seasonal conditions to grow and thrive. Ecclesiastes 3:1–2 tells us, "There is a time for everything, and everything on earth has its special season. There is a time to be born and a time to die. There is a time to plant and a time to pull up plants."

We talked about the types of flowers she would like to plant. Tulips are bulbs that need to be planted in the fall to grow in the spring.

My friend and I discussed a few plants she would like to grow in a garden for her family to eat. Blackberries are wonderful but require space to grow their trailing vines. Tomatoes work great in small spaces. Strawberries prefer well-drained soil and need full sun. The best time to plant tomatoes in Kansas is between April and May.

God lovingly gave you the example of timing when He created the purpose of the four seasons to be a part of the earth (Psalm 74:17). Spring, summer, autumn, and winter repetitively determine the process of weather, hours of daylight, and ecology throughout the year.

God established the cycle of seasons after the flood, vowing never again to curse the ground because of human beings (Genesis 8:21). The consistency of the seasons reminds you of God's constant connectedness, faithfulness, and sovereignty.

Weather changes each season, causing plants, animals, and people to adjust their behaviors and focus. You and I change and adapt, but God doesn't need to. God is the same, connected in all seasons (Acts 14:17).

In scripture, God uses the seasons as an example of the process and changes we all experience in our beliefs throughout our lives (Daniel 2:21). God fixes, arranges, and manages the seasons. He promises to walk with you every season of life, providing peace.

The movement of the sun, moon, and stars reflects the earth's rotation and provides the basic standards for the calendar, Britannica.com explains. Your day can be measured by the stars or the sun. The month is established by the earth's passage around the world. A year is the time the earth takes to complete an orbit around the sun.

Calendars were created after our ancestors studied the timing of night patterns in the sky and learned about the passing of migrating animals. They depended on calendars to know when to plant crops, when their livestock would give birth, and when to hunt certain wild animals.

Calendars are essential to people. Nowadays, we use our calendars only to book meetings, plan vacations, and plan events that don't involve a connection with nature or being outside.

The timing of your day is the same as everyone else's. The day begins as the sun rises and ends as it sets. God made the sun to be loyal and very dependable. You can set your watch to the sun's schedule anytime.

Each day begins with a connection to the process of time. Your alarm wakes you. After you crawl out of bed, it is time to eat breakfast, the first meal. You might be seated at a table and chair made from a tree God grew and harvested at the right time for the wood to create your furniture.

Maybe you are wearing a cotton shirt or shorts made from plants God created to be harvested and processed to make your clothing. God's incredible timing gave life to the seed that grew the coffee beans harvested and processed at just the right moment to be used in your precious cup of delicious coffee.

The wheat field grown to make your toast was harvested at just the right time to be ground into flour. The strawberries were picked at just the right time to make the jam for your toast. The oranges were picked at just the right time to make orange juice. By now, you are grasping how God's timing in nature affects every minute of your day at just the right time.

God is always with you, watching over and taking care of you whether you acknowledge Him or not, because that is the loving God that He is.

Next time you wonder where God is, step back and look at the overall big picture (Psalm 115:2). Logically think about the purpose and process of God's connection to the timing of everything perfectly created for you to have food. Think about the magnitude of timing and planning God has orchestrated for the rest of your day! Maybe your question will change to, "Where isn't God?"

God has a purpose for His plan and encourages you to be patient, knowing He will work things out in His time, not yours. God knows exactly what you need and when you need it.

Don't worry about what everyone else thinks. God created you and will always love you. Even if you mess up, nothing is a mistake if you see it as an opportunity. Follow God's plan and do what you know is right and true.

Life on earth is a process based on timing and compiling the description of your experiences. The schools you have attended, the towns and neighborhoods you have lived in, and your family and friends all shape and mold you into who you are.

You can step out of your box and look at the big picture; every event, accomplishment, and encounter cultivates your perspective and how you see things. You will see the whole process, all the connections, and what their purpose is meant to accomplish.

Society teaches you to expect everything now, to have it at your fingertips. Friend, God designed nothing about life on this earth to be instantaneous.

The sun follows a path to rise and set, the water cycle is slow and continual, and the dung beetle spends its entire life creating healthy soil. You will experience the foundational meaning of why you were made throughout the timing of events in your life.

You are an integral part of God's orderly plan for creation, constantly connected to nature. If you live life expecting people, relationships, situations, and life events to provide what you want instantaneously, you will be continually disappointed.

The process of time is the backbone of creating life cycle experiences. In every season, nature ensures that all resources are thoroughly used.

Nature circles around many processes for a purpose. Living your life is about God's timing and how you get where He wants you to be. The repetitive system works because people are programmed to be outcome orientated. If you let it, looking and committing yourself to the process will transform your life and solidify the change.

God's created timing of nature provides an example for you and me to follow. The order of nature's process aligns with our lives.

Albert Einstein was not a believer. Yet when he contemplated the wonders of the universe, he respected that there must be a God. When asked if he was an atheist, his reply was no.

Life revolves around steps, seasons, and order. Sometimes, the season changes just when I think I am getting a handle on life. New things are continually thrown our way.

Looking at the overall picture, the timing of life begins when you are born. As a baby, your parents care for you, providing for your every need and want. Animals care for and teach their young as well (Psalm 91:4).

As time progresses, you continually develop and learn to adjust. Old enough to attend school, day after day, year after year, you journey through the educational system, growing bigger each year like trees. Graduation confirms you are ready to conquer the world and become an adult, much like baby birds learning to use their wings for the first time and fly.

Finding a mate can be a timely, soul-searching process. When starting a family, you watch your kids grow over time. Then the time comes for you to take care of your parents. Soon after, your kids begin to take care of you. It seems the season changes just when you think you have life all figured out.

One day, you realize you can't seem to do the physical things you used to do. The body's aging is a gradual process occurring over time (2 Corinthians 5:1). The eyes can't see quite so well, and the ears can't hear as much anymore. Sometimes, I think this might actually be a blessing in disguise.

When I put my glasses on and get really close to the mirror, I see wrinkles, brown spots, and hair that make me look much older than I think I am. Seeing my chin up close makes me wonder if I am related to a goat.

You and I get older every day when the sun rises (Job 14:1–2). Over time, our skin ages and sags, muscles aren't as strong as they once were, and our body doesn't move like it used to (Job 14:10–12). You might not be there yet, but someday you will.

We can see the repetitive body aging process occurring in people, elephants, trees, and rocks. Maybe God makes the eyes deteriorate so we can't see the aging process quite so well. Our minds might feel more comfortable because of what we can't see.

Over the years, people can become much wiser (Job 12:12–13). Listen to their amazing stories as they share information and insight.

"People treat you like a queen when you are 90. They respect you because you are old. But in your head, you have not changed. You think you are still young" (Betty White).

Do you know someone happy to share and pass along wisdom gleaned from their many years? I love listening to stories told by folks who have lived longer than I have.

Older people should be cherished and honored. Just like trees have golden colors when the leaves are aging, people have golden years as they age.

Your wrinkles are a sign of wisdom and maturity. Allow your perspective to accept the noticeable timing and changes in your life. Be proud of your wrinkles; you have earned them. Enjoy the creation that God made you to be. He loves you and thinks you look perfect.

The Lord has a plan for when we age. Isaiah 54:10 expresses the steadfastness of God's promise: "The mountains may disappear, and the hills may come to an end, but my love will never disappear; my promise of peace will not come to an end." This reminds us of God's unwavering commitment to you and me that His love for us will never change.

As the seasons of life change, your purpose may change as well, but God will never leave you. Friend, that is how the timing of life happens. Wrap your mind around it so you can let go of your fears and live a peaceful life accordingly.

It can be overwhelming and exhausting to think about the timing of all the systems and processes necessary to make this planet function. But don't worry. There is no need to.

God created all this and will never leave you. He has a plan, and you can trust Him. Even though your body is becoming older, the spirit inside you is new every day (2 Corinthians 4:16).

There will always be things you cannot control that might make you fearful or sad (2 Corinthians 7:10), which is why God made His presence in nature so obvious. If you look for and recognize it, you will see His presence in the sunshine after the rain (Ephesians 1:11).

The timing of life changes can be complicated and scary, but God always comforts us. God can use trials in life to draw you closer while you depend on and believe in Him.

"I have made you pure, but not by fire, as silver I made pure. I have purified you by giving you troubles. I do this for myself, for my own sake. I will not let people speak evil against me or let some god take my glory" (Isaiah 48:10–11).

With a gratified perspective, unhappy times can make you thankful for the good times in life. How will you help others if you have never experienced troubles (2 Corinthians 1:3–4)?

You will always be able to look back in time and see God's presence guiding you through your trials so you can pass that kind of comfort along to others in the future.

Where will you be in one hundred years? Did you know your grandpa's dad? What do you know about him? What will others remember about you? What kind of legacy will you leave for your family?

We all have the same twenty-four hours in a day, but it's how we spend those minutes that make a difference. Currently, what are you doing with your one precious, God-given life on this earth to make it matter?

When you choose God, you become more at peace with the timing of your circumstances. You will never clearly hear God if you don't allow Him into your heart.

Do you recognize the presence and voice of your Creator, the one who has saved you (Isaiah 48:17)?

What are you waiting for?

Points to Ponder

Do you embrace God's plan?

CHAPTER 15

WHEN YOU LOOK FOR GOD, HE GETS EASIER TO SEE

Is every day the same when you wake up each morning? Of course not.

Each morning, the sun declares a new day triumphantly with an entrance of striking colors. As light awakens the world, you crawl out of bed to embark on your new God-gifted experience.

You might initiate the day by showering, making coffee, or cooking breakfast. You could crack open a few eggs, fry some bacon, or pour orange juice to fill your rumbling tummy. While doing all this, do you think about God's creation plan? Or just your to-do list for the day and everything that needs to be accomplished.

God's organizational plan is so ingrained in our everyday lives that we no longer see it. In the first chapter of Genesis, God outlines His design and explains it as He created it. God names and gives us the words for each aspect and step in the plan.

Since creation began, that plan has stayed the same. God's descriptions in the Bible are not just empty and meaningless words on a page. Walk around and look outside at nature. The very planet we live on constantly revolves around the plan explained in God's Word.

Do you ever consider how plants that continually grow from seeds provide food for everything living?

The Bible explains that people are responsible for caring for land and animals. God's wild and tame animals continually help people and the ecosystem function.

God's creative processes repetitively connect with everything you do, from when you wake up in the morning to when you go to bed at night.

The sun lights your way to see and tells you what time it is. God designed cows to produce your morning go-to drink, apples for juice, and wheat for toast. God makes water to help you smell better, provide moisture for your garden, and help the package you ordered online get delivered to your door. Plants create oxygen for you to breathe and allow your body to function. The list of how nature affects your life goes on and on.

God created a beautiful world for you and me to show His abundant goodness and kindness (Psalm 50:2). God wasn't required to make the universe; He wanted to. Nature displays God's love so you can connect with Him and see His presence on earth (Psalm 115:16).

What parts of the day do you welcome God into your daily life schedule? Do you talk to God or pray before you eat? Do you take the time to read a devotion? Look to see God's hand in your current situation and thank Him.

God is in control, and you are not (Deuteronomy 10:17–18). Sometimes, people can make life so hard on themselves, trying to make it more complex than it should be.

God's plan isn't difficult to understand. You continually breathe, drink, eat, and literally stand on it. You speak and sing about nature daily without even thinking about it. You are the apple of His eye.

God's creation aims to highlight His presence and profess His glory. "There are things about him that people cannot see—his eternal power and all the things that make him God. But since the beginning of the world, those things have been easy to understand by what God has made. So, people have no excuse for their bad actions" (Romans 1:20).

Do you believe in the presence of God that you see before you in nature? Let your faith germinate in the Almighty Creator. Confidently live life with faith, walking with God in His perfect timing, believing in His glorious presence that you see.

When your eyes see a zebra's black-and-white stripes, your mind connects and knows that it is a zebra. When your eyes see Jesus's name written in black on a white page, your mind recognizes His name as the Son of God.

Why do we automatically trust the doctor to tell us how to make our bodies better? We trust the plumber to do whatever he needs to fix our leaking sink and the guy at the mechanic shop to stop the awful noise from under the hood of our car.

Yet, we constantly question and doubt the power of our heavenly Father, the Creator of the universe, who made and gifted the doctor, plumber, and mechanic.

Even though Jesus walked on this earth two thousand years ago, people still recognize and honor His name. Just seeing or hearing His name causes one to feel wonder and amazement.

God's power comes from who He is, not what we call Him (Revelation 1:8). Throughout the world, people use different names from the Bible for God and Jesus. We may speak the names differently and use them in various contexts, but who they represent is the same.

Jesus is the Son of God wherever you are in His crafted universe. He knows who you are and where you are on His created earth (1 Samuel 16:7).

You can read about His ultimate power on display throughout His holy Word (1 Chronicles 29:11). The Bible speaks of miracles and how God provided for His people using nature, and it describes mystical events that changed the course of a typical day.

Have you ever read the story of Lazarus? Just before Jesus raised Martha's brother from the dead, He told her, "Didn't I tell you that if you believed, you would see the glory of God?" (John 11:40).

Not one person will be able to stand before God and state that they did not receive His revelation through His creation.

Like nature, everything in and about life constantly and repetitively evolves each season. Living life is a lot like the weather. The process of change is a good thing and affects everyone. The key to change is learning how you can manage it.

The process of life changing can be intimidating. How do you process the changing seasons of life?

Hezekiah prayed, and God listened. Answering Hezekiah's prayer, God added fifteen years to his life. To show God would do what he said, He provided a sign. The process of a shadow made by the sun on the stairway of Ahaz went back up ten steps (2 Kings 20:8–11). God's presence erases fear and is always available to those who trust Him.

Do you like change in your life? If you have lived a few years, you should know that the only thing constant is change. God created you to be a constant work in progress as your purpose changes.

Everyone has the same 86,400 seconds in a day. Most of us

make decisions based on what we already know and repetitively waste time thinking about things we can't change.

By planning your time better, you won't waste it. Instead, take a walk outside and breathe in some fresh air. Pause to think and pray about the process of the new situation. How might it affect your future and help grow your faith?

This is the second marriage for both my farmer husband and me. We have nine children together and make it a point to continually work on our marriage.

So we traveled to Colorado for a week of marriage counseling. If you aren't working to grow together in a marriage, you are growing apart, right?

During the week, we concentrated on chipping away bad habits and removing old baggage from previous relationships. Can you relate? Everyone is carrying some baggage.

On the last day, my morning devotion was written by a friend going through marital issues. The message was perfect and seemed to have been written just for us.

In the lesson, Lysa shared details about visiting Michelangelo's *David* in Italy and how the different sculptures in the exhibit made her feel. We then shared the devotion with our counselor and were reminded that each of us is a masterpiece created by God. God will gently chip away the rough edges if we are willing, sculpting you and me into the person He wants us to be.

Three days later, back at home, my mom and sister came to visit. We were shopping in a small Kansas town of about seven hundred people. I looked to my right while waiting in line at a lovely dress shop. Staring at me eye to eye was a white ceramic bust of *David*. I was shocked and excited!

Immediately, I reached over to get him. Upon closer inspection, he was a bank. The figurine was perfect and on sale.

Now *David* sits in our bedroom on top of the chest of drawers. The sound of coins dropping into the bank reminds us of how God repetitively chips away at our old baggage, forming us into His new masterpiece.

Each living thing, including you and me, changes and matures as it grows and develops. Individual organisms are born, live, and die; new ones replace them to ensure the species' survival.

Every living organism in nature has a series of changes or a life cycle. An insect's life cycle differs from that of a bird, plant, or animal, just like the journey of each human life is different.

The life of a fly ranges from fifteen to thirty days, while that of a redwood tree can last eight hundred to fifteen hundred years. My husband's grandfather passed away six weeks shy of his 108th birthday.

How does each season of life look to you with every candle added to your birthday cake? Adding candles doesn't seem nearly as exciting as when I was waiting to reach double digits. However, each year of life becomes much more appreciated and treasured.

Follow nature's lead by trusting God wholeheartedly (Psalm 20:7). Trees, flowers, birds, and bears all trust Him to provide what they need to survive. God continually takes care of them and you.

The miracle of nature germinates your faith, teaching you to believe in what you see. Nature is designed perfectly. God not only creates repetitively but continues to oversee the entire process.

When King David was a boy, his days were spent herding his family's sheep in nature's wilderness. His home was outdoors. David witnessed God's glory in creation daily with each new sunrise, in the meadow's beautiful green grass, and the blue sky above with white, puffy clouds.

"The heavens declare the glory of God; the skies proclaim the work of His hands" (Psalms 19:1). King David got it. He knew His Creator and gave God the glory.

David wrote, "You made my whole being. You formed me in my mother's body. I praise you because you made me in an amazing and wonderful way. What you have done is wonderful. I know this very well. You saw my bones being formed as I took shape in my mother's body. When I was put together there, you saw my body as it was formed. All the days planned for me were written in your book before I was one day old" (Psalm 139:13–16).

I like to think of David as a big brother because I genuinely get where he comes from. I grew up working outside on a farm daily. Can you relate? Do you love being outside?

- I see God in the tiny corn seeds that germinate, growing to be ten-foot-tall plants while reproducing themselves six hundred times over.

- I see God's presence in the baby goat trying out new legs and searching for its mother's milk, who was curled up in his mother's womb only minutes before.

- I see God's mighty presence in the beautiful, thundering, life-giving rain clouds I fervently prayed for.

Trusting in God's amazing glory is easy when I can see, touch, and smell it.

My simple farm girl perspective aligns with David's. Those of us whose livelihood depends upon nature and God believe in the miracles described in the Bible because we continually witness them in nature. Faith germinates from the miracles we see growing and thriving around us.

I find it fascinating that King David, the man after God's heart, lived almost three thousand years ago. Yet God gave Michelangelo the passion and talent 2,500 years later to carve a seventeen-foot statue of His good friend David. Five hundred years after the statue was finished, it still stands in Florence, Italy.

Today, you and I can still see the masterpiece for ourselves. The carving of *David* is a fantastic work of art. Michelangelo outdid himself, forming incredible details. But I wonder if we have missed the reason God had the statue created in the first place.

When David realized he had messed up, he would ask God with his whole heart for forgiveness. David wasn't perfect; he was far from ideal. But neither am I. God used David as an example of someone after His own heart. David was the kind of person God wants you and me to be.

Maybe God commissioned the statue as a tangible reminder of the relationship you and I can have with Him (Psalm 89:35–37). God wants you and me to search for His heart, just as David did continually.

Even though you might mess up, God doesn't go anywhere. It doesn't matter what you did or might have said. God loves you and wants to connect anyway.

Doesn't thinking about David's relationship with God make you smile? David was far from perfect, but God still forgave and loved him. God is waiting to do the same for you.

When you think about creation, how is it designed to connect, flow, and work together flawlessly? God made the process of nature to express His love to you. Nature doesn't need you to do anything. However, you need nature just like you need God.

What is your story with God? Is He your friend? Do you share His love with others?

A connect group at my church was discussing how God could use regular people like you and me to share His love.

Our homework assignment was to pray that God would show us how to help others that week. So on a trip with my farmer husband to pick up purchased equipment several states away, I prayed that God would use me to bless others.

I almost didn't remember the jacket I had left on the back of my chair as we left the hotel on the second day of our voyage. Walking back into the breakfast area, I saw a man waving to get my attention.

Speaking excitedly in broken English, the man explained that he had always wondered what the little packets on the counter contained. Watching me make my breakfast, he was thrilled to learn it was oatmeal.

He wished me a blessed day and thanked me several times for my help. I felt incredibly humbled and almost confused as I walked away from an answer to my prayer.

Later in the day, we stopped at a restaurant. A sweet, older lady in the restroom pulled me aside to explain how she learned to "finagle" the soap dispenser by observing me wash my hands. She wanted to thank me for helping her.

We chatted, and I wished her a blessed day. I couldn't help but smile and soak in her presence. She was the second answer to my prayer.

I will be candid and admit that when I prayed to be a blessing to someone, I thought it would be some valiant action God would assign me to do for them. The answer to my prayer wasn't at all what I had expected.

It was overwhelming to realize that other people are watching every "normal" daily task I do and how God uses that. Friend, you are being watched as well. How we react to those who share our lives can make a massive difference to them.

But isn't that just like God and nature? When you think you might be getting things figured out, God shows you something new. He always teaches you how to show His glory to others if you pay attention.

Get to know God. Connect and have a one-on-one personal relationship with Him. God is always beside you and will never leave (1 Timothy 2:5–6).

You can talk to God as you would a friend because He is your friend. That is how God designed your relationship with Him.

My aunt Marion always said, "To have a friend, you must be a friend." In any relationship, you must learn to converse and get to know the other person.

God wants to share His wisdom with you, but you must repetitively listen to His voice speaking to your heart. Can you just sit and be without doing anything? Try to be still, sit near some flowers, breathe in their sweet aroma, process, and listen to what God wants to tell you.

Sit outside in the sunshine and soak in God's peace. Your one precious life will function much smoother with God's guidance.

You can connect with God through nature by looking for all the details He created. The bright red color of the tiny ladybug and the spectacular patterns of birds flying in the air are easy to appreciate. Marvel at viewing the vastness of the snowcapped mountains.

Try reading the remarkable hidden ways of God in the Bible, His holy Word, to learn more about Him. BIBLE = Believers' Instructions Before Leaving Earth.

Instead of focusing on how the scripture applies to you, look for and understand the Almighty Creator's behaviors, likes, and dislikes and what makes Him tick. God explains how He wants you to live your one life if you study and live out His words.

"God's handiwork is visible all around us, but His greatest work is our salvation, which He provided through the sacrifice of His Son, Jesus" (Dr. Charles F. Stanley).

"God loved the world so much that He gave His one and only Son so that whoever believes in Him may not be lost but have eternal life" (John 3:16).

In the beginning, God created with Jesus and for Jesus. "This is what real love is: It is not our love for God; it is God's love for us in sending His Son to be the way to take away our sins" (1 John 4:10).

Is Jesus your friend and savior? Do you have a relationship with Him?

God wants you to be more like His Son, Jesus, and will continually work with you to make this happen. It's a process that begins when you confess your sins to Jesus and culminates with you spending eternity with Him face-to-face (Phil. 3:21).

"If you know that Christ is all that is right, you know that all who do right are God's children" (1 John 2:29).

Jesus understands the process of dealing with family and friends' judgments. He walked this earth as a human for thirty-three years and can help you live your life.

The Son of the Living God has experienced blisters on His feet and rocks in his sandals. He knows how it feels when friends are mad at you for not doing what they want.

Jesus dealt with His anxiety while trying to have a solid relationship with His earthly parents and family, which probably caused him some sleepless nights. Our Savior understands living life on earth because He chose to fulfill His heavenly Father's plan.

Before Jesus died, leading priests and teachers of the law repetitively made fun of Him by pronouncing that Jesus saved other people but could not save himself. "If He is really the

Christ, the king of Israel, let him come down now from the cross. When we see this, we will believe in him" (Mark 15:32).

Nature confirmed the magnitude of Jesus's death. The sun stopped shining around noon. The whole land was dark until three o'clock in the afternoon (Luke 23:44–46), the exact time Jesus cried out His last words loudly and died.

In my simple little mind, I sometimes wonder how creation felt about watching Jesus die that day. Hanging on a cross made from a tree that He designed, Jesus died for all our sins.

When the beautiful sunshine He originated was high in the sky, watching its beloved Creator suffer, it must have been very sad. It stopped working, fearful of what was happening to the author of life. God allowed the process of the sun to go dark.

The curtain in the Temple tore from top to bottom into two pieces. The earth that Jesus formed shook as rocks split and broke apart, forcing the people watching to realize Jesus was indeed the Son of God. Only then did the hard-hearted people who mocked Jesus truly comprehend what they had just done.

You and I might tell ourselves to believe only when we see it, but God tells us the opposite. He said to them, "Because of your little faith. For truly, I say to you, if you have faith like a grain of mustard seed, you will say to this mountain, 'Move from here to there,' and it will move, and nothing will be impossible for you" (Matthew 17:20).

Faith is a process that can often grow out of desperation and fear. Remember that faith doesn't take you out of the problem but through it.

You are blessed because you can see the presence of God through nature during your fears, continually building your faith. Take a walk through God's incredible creation. See God's presence with your own eyes and ears. Talk to Him directly about your problems, constantly germinating more faith to walk through life.

When Jesus was in Galilee, a king's officer begged him to come and heal his son. "Jesus said to him, 'You people must see signs and miracles before you will believe in me.'" The man believed, and the son was healed.

Even though Jesus had performed countless miraculous signs and wonders, many people still did not believe in Him (John 12:37).

"Faith is visualizing the future. It's believing before you see it" (Pastor Rick Warren).

Michelangelo's faith propelled him into carving on a seventeen-foot block of stone. Night and day, for three years, he worked to create a resemblance of God's good friend David out of marble. God gifted the artist with a vision of the final product. The sculptor was fearless and believed what the block of stone could be before anyone else could see it.

Do you know anyone with faith like that? Have you experienced faith that allowed you to visualize the future before seeing it?

When you give your life to Jesus, you let go of fear and believe He is real. "Where God's love is, there is no fear, because God's perfect love drives out fear. It is punishment that makes a person fear, so love is not made perfect in the person who fears" (1 John 4:18).

Germinating your faith pleases God. "Whoever confesses that Jesus is the Son of God has God living inside, and that person lives in God. And so, we know the love that God has for us, and we trust that love" (1 John 4:15–16).

Faith will help you believe that God made the entire world (Romans 10:17). Nature's flowers, clouds, dogs, and rocks are just a few creations you see repetitively that help you to believe they are created by something that cannot be seen (2 Corinthians 4:18).

Your faith in Jesus will help you conquer the world (1 John 5:4). Walking through the storms of life with Him will only strengthen you.

"It was by faith that Noah heard God's warnings about things he could not yet see. He obeyed God and built a large boat to save his family. By his faith, Noah showed that the world was wrong, and he became one of those made right with God through faith" (Hebrews 11:7).

When you give your heart to Jesus, your spirit will come to life and function as God designed it to. Jesus is the only way that you will ever be able to see God. Knowing Jesus, your heart will be satisfied and search no more.

I'm amazed that someone so important is interested in you and me. Why does He even care about the timing of the little details of our lives? He has the process of an entire universe to care for, yet He takes the time to listen to our prayers.

After Job focused on God and His power instead of his weakness, he could be honest with himself and God. Job could admit that he had been acting unwisely.

Your belief in God will determine your relationship with Him and your thoughts. Choosing God will make you far more at peace with your current circumstances (Hebrews 10:22). "We live by what we believe, not by what we can see" (2 Corinthians 5:7).

From the beginning of Job's story, he was straightforward with God. He expressed his hurt and disappointment out loud for everyone to hear. Job never tried to pretend that everything was okay and that he wasn't struggling.

If you don't have enough faith to trust God, tell Him. Humility is knowing when to own it and admitting you are wrong. God offers actual life change. The question is, do you want it? Do you really want the change you are looking for?

Is your lack of trust caused by something you don't understand? Tell God about your struggle, deal with the issue, and get it out in the open so that you can conquer it. Allow your perspective to be refocused.

Are you comfortable with your broken life? Are you willing to be uncomfortable in making a change? "My ears had heard of you, but now my eyes have seen you" (Job 42:5).

We can't see beyond the moment we live, but God can. Are you focused on God's purpose for where you are and looking for His presence in creation near you? Brokenness will not have the last word. The beauty of perfect wholeness will.

God's faithfulness prepares you for the process and purpose of what is ahead. Can you trust that you are right where God wants you to be? The Almighty Creator is the only source that can and will satisfy the repetitive longing of your desperate soul.

You won't be able to move forward until you understand the process of your past and learn from your healing accomplishments. The gift of memory is repetitively remembering God's unfailing faithfulness and His enduring, unfailing love.

Write down where you see God daily in your God's Presence Diary so you can look back through the pages in times of distress and remember how faithful He is. This will help you move forward confidently, releasing your fears and knowing God's desire is for you.

What do you look for? Do you repetitively see the signs of God in nature before you?

Do you believe in the glory of the Almighty Creator that you can focus on? Once you recognize the beauty and glory of God in nature, it is something you can't unsee.

The signs of God are repetitively placed before you. By

loving God, you will see His beauty everywhere.

You might witness the sunrise from the east daily, watch a hawk circle effortlessly across the beautiful blue sky, or hear the rumblings of thunder before a storm. Do you give God credit and glory when you see a colorful rainbow in the sky? God has authority over all the earth.

God knows your heart because He created it. The heart is a dwelling place for God's spirit and determines your perspective.

What is in your heart determines how frequently you will see the sunshine in God's timely presence, how often you allow His presence to live daily with you, and how regularly you let God guide the process of choosing your purpose of love. God longs for you to make Him a priority and love Him as much as He loves you.

Creation is a Process. Connecting its Purpose of Repeating God's love and presence over and over for you to see without fear. PCPR is being still and knowing that He is God (Psalm 46:10). Learn to appreciate God's presence everywhere in creation and thank Him for never leaving you alone (Deuteronomy 31:6).

Let go of your fears and find your purpose through God's creation. Nature is a universal testimony displayed to everyone on the earth, continually night and day. The power of God declared through His handiwork is unmistakable. Nature provides obvious and explicit details of God's plan if your heart is willing to believe in what you see.

God, the author of life, is a permanent solution to your problems.

TIPS FOR USING NATURE TO RELAX

In the previous chapters, you learned that God designed people to be part of and united with creation.

You are blessed with five senses that physically connect you with nature: taste, touch, sight, smell, and sound. The Almighty Creator connected you with nature in a special way.

Nature and your senses have an excellent partnership that works together for your gratification.

"How many are your works, Lord! In wisdom, you made them all; the earth is full of your creatures" (Psalm 104:24).

No matter where you are on this earth, people want to see and hear the peaceful hums and rhythms that God-created water makes. We are drawn to the soothing sounds water creates. Listening to its melody seems to relax every cell of your being.

Jesus understands what your body needs and doesn't because He created you. That is why He provides colorful flowers, fresh oxygen from trees, dancing butterflies, the welcoming comfort of warm sunshine, the relaxing blue sky, animal friends, and many other things for you to enjoy the healing nature of creation.

With your senses, you can truly indulge in every characteristic nature offers. The beauty of nature alone nourishes your mind, body, soul, and the very core of your being. Submerge yourself in the great outdoors. Your body will become stronger, and your mind will rid itself of unwanted, unneeded stress.

Nature offers many ways to relax. Below is a list that highlights only ten of them!

1. Go outside and take a walk. Look for beauty and bathe your soul in God's glory.

2. Suck in a big breath of oxygenated air. Let it fill every cell in your body and just be. Relax.

3. Close your eyes and truly feel the warm sunshine on your skin.

4. Look for and enjoy the sights of the big and small. Marvel that each has an individual purpose.

5. Listen to many different sounds. What is making the sound?

6. Close your eyes and smell the different aromas. Where are they coming from?

7. Look around and identify as many amazing textures as you can. Feel them.

8. Watch the sunrise. How many colors did you see?

9. Visit a zoo or farm. Hang out with the animals and watch how they interact.

10. Sit beside a body of water and experience the calming qualities. Neurochemicals in your brain will rejoice.

Grounding

Living life can be challenging at times. While trying to cope with an anxiety attack, test your five senses. If you feel you have lost all control of your surroundings, try this method called grounding.

1. In your mind, count five things you can see.

2. Then count four things you can touch.

3. Three things you can hear.

4. Two things you can smell.

5. One thing you can taste.

Grounding will help you to stay focused and learn to use nature to help you live life. Go outside and take advantage of the peaceful, soothing, comforting opportunities God has blessed you with on this earth through nature.

God created for six days and rested on the seventh, providing an example for us to follow. Remember the sabbath day and keep it holy (Exodus 20:8–11). There is an old saying in the farming community: work on Sunday, fix on Monday.

Rest is essential for the body. Lack of sleep can cause many problems and affect countless aspects of life. "Be still, and know that I am God," Psalm 46:10 says.

Learning to enjoy the outdoors and nature provides many positive attributes. Nature is calm, reduces stress, and provides energy, which helps with weight loss and makes you happy.

Paddle boats; Pete's Puddle, August 1979

Logs and slide

Grandpa, Grandma, and me, 1987

Grandpa in tractor inner tube

Cutting silo feed in 1986

Haymonster

ABOUT THE AUTHOR

Born a farmer's daughter, Debbie is blessed to be a farmer's wife. Her favorite place is outside, soaking up the sunshine while inhaling fresh, oxygenated air. Working with nature to provide food for people and livestock has always been her passion.

She holds degrees in animal science and agricultural economics from Kansas State University and deeply appreciates that God is a part of everything created.

Debbie's perception of God and nature differs from that of someone who has always lived in a town or big city. Creation is and has always been such a huge part of her life.

She enjoys taking pictures of the beautiful scenery in the Flint Hills of Kansas, where she lives with her farmer husband in their empty nest. The natural beauty is a continual reminder of God's daily miracles.

Striving to share her perspective with children, young people, and you, Debbie wants to inspire a daily connection with God through the secrets of nature so that each person will have their own intimate, personal relationship with the Almighty Creator, the one whose image you bear.

Connect with Debbie on Facebook at Go Experience Nature Now, Instagram at go.experience.nature1, or check out her website at www.GoExperienceNature.com.